WHAT IS A MAN?
Workbook

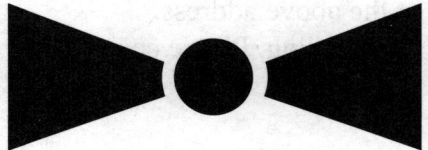

Dr. Joaquin G. Molina

Copyright © 2015 by Dr. Joaquin G. Molina

All rights reserved. No part of this publication may be reproduced, distributed or transmitted in any form or by any means, including photocopying, recording, or other electronic or mechanical, without permission that was pre-written and the publisher's consent, except in the case of brief quotations in critical reviews and other noncommercial uses permitted by copyright law. For requests for permission, write to the publisher, addressed "Attention: Permissions Coordinator," at the address below.
What Is A Man? Workbook P. O. Box 654338
Miami, Florida 33265 www.solmiami.org

Acknowledgment for layout format and revision: Dr. Jules and Claudia Molina

Ordering Information: Permission to Use Copyright
Please contact the Permissions Department if you desire to use an extract or copyright material of evidence of Dr. Joaquin G. Molina on a non-exclusive basis in book format only. Please direct your inquiry in writing to:

Spring of Life Fellowship
Attn: S.O.L. Media Dept.
P. O. Box 654338 Miami, Florida 33265
Or fax your request on official letterhead to:
(305) 597- 4447

I.S.B.N. : 978-0-9746329-8-8

Unless otherwise noted, all biblical texts are taken from the King James Version of the Holy Bible. Used with permission under Gratis Use & Fair Use Guidelines.

Sales amount. Special discounts on quantity purchases by corporations, associations, and others. For more information, please contact the editor at the above address.
Ordering bookstores and wholesalers U.S. trading. Please contact the retailer:
Tel.: (305) 597-4440
Fax: (305) 597-4447
Or visit www.whatisaman.com

Impreso en Colombia - Printed in Colombia

SMALL GROUP COMMITMENT

As you begin this study, it is important that your small group commit together in agreement to journey through the quest to manhood. Once this commitment is acknowledged and agreed upon, your What is a Man? small group will be on its way to experience true Christian Community. It is so important that your small group discuss these values before you begin this quest. Start a quick review of these terms and sign your name as a physical reminder of your commitment.

PRIORITY: While we are in this small group, we will give our small group highest and top priority.

PARTICIPATION: Everyone is encouraged to participate and no one dominates the discussions.

RESPECT: Every one is given a right to his own opinion, and all questions are encouraged and respected.

CONFIDENTIALITY: Anything that is said in our meetings is never repeated outside the meetings without permission.

LIFE CHANGE: The men will regularly assess progress by taking steps of obedience to God's Word and apply the principles discovered in their quest to manhood.

CARE AND SUPPORT: Permission is given so the men in the small groups may call the leader and request help from one another by asking for prayer and help in tough times.

ACCOUNTABILITY: We agree to open our lives as men to our small groups and live transparently by permitting other men to speak godly counsel into our lives without offence.

MISSION: The mission for every small group is to seek and save the lost man while they grow in manhood to reach out to other men in every direction so they also could benefit and grow.

MINISTRY: This is a ministry for men that are willing to serve God and others by giving of their time, talents and treasure to further the quest toward manhood.

I, _____, agree to all of the above. Date: _____
       (YOUR NAME)

TABLE OF CONTENTS

ABOUT THE AUTHOR 5
AUTHOR'S NOTE 6
THE QUEST FOR MANHOOD EXPERIENCE 7

SESSION 1 8
Understanding: What is a Man?

SESSION 2 19
Jesus Christ the Perfect Model of a Man

SESSION 3 27
Man as Spirit, Soul, and Body

SESSION 4 40
Thoughts, Words, and Actions

SESSION 5 51
Time, Talents, and Treasures

SESSION 6 62
Faithfulness: The Cornerstone of Character

SESSION 7 74
Godly Man or Peter Pan

SESSION 8 88
Finally a Man

SESSION 9 101
Love vs. Self

CONCLUSION 115

DECLARATION OF MANHOOD 118

LEADER NOTES 119

ABOUT THE AUTHOR

For the past 30 years, Dr. Joaquin G. Molina has taken an extraordinary journey in the pursuit of discovering the depth, significance, and reality of the issues pertaining to manhood. Through unique and profound personal experiences, the author has traced the Biblical pathways and is now able to reveal the hidden treasures that establish a foundation to combat the manhood crisis. This most recent publication, "What is a Man? Workbook" is the final compilation of serious information and techniques combined with intense passion and practical insight that will allow men the opportunity to begin their quest in search for true manhood.

Dr. Molina is a prominent leader among the Body of Christ, in addition to serving as keynote speaker in many forums both National and International conferences as a respected author. His passion is to see the character of men transformed and begin leading their families and local churches. Dr. Joaquin G. Molina is most distinguished among his peers for his compelling wisdom, insight, and delivery of powerful Biblical truths and convictions on the vital issues confronting the church and family such as lack of integrity, divorce, fatherlessness, broken marriages, and broken family.

He presently presides as senior pastor and founder of Spring of Life Fellowship Church in Miami, Florida where he serves accompanied by his wife Yvette and four children: Nicholas, Joshua, Brandon and Christina.

A WORD FROM THE AUTHOR

Most men will proclaim each his own goodness, But who can find a faithful man?
Proverbs 20:6

The ultimate measure of a true man is not where he stands in ordinary moments of fun and entertainment but in the crossroads of life, when challenged by controversy of truth and defending what is right. A true man chooses to act courageously with strength of integrity in the face of difficult situations. His priority is to serve and protect the welfare of his loved ones and to defend them against all potential harm. A real man will do anything necessary to leave a legacy of blessing to his family. He stands ready to demonstrate full capacity to protect his family and defend them at all times regardless of the cost, whether it requires the loss of his prestige, popularity, fame, fortune, or anything else that could compromise the principles and convictions he holds as true.

The attitudes and expressions of those who pursue genuine manhood may often offend others, especially those who conform to a life of perpetual wanderings in a holding pattern of immaturity and spiritual mediocrity. The tragedy becomes evident when men would prefer to avoid the personal responsibility of growing towards maturity because they realize that the pursuit of manhood is either too costly or challengingly difficult. Instead, they prefer to travel down an easier road, one of leisure and fantasy (avoiding reality), holding on to a state of lifelong immaturity. When real life confronts these men and their continual infantile imaginations, they respond with same childish tantrums and fanciful rebellion. Similar to the cartoon character known as Peter Pan, they simply refuse to grow up.

It is my hope and prayer that soon all men will realize that the only pathway toward the full measure and stature of a true man is Christ and Christ alone.

Dr. Joaquin G. Molina
-World Changer

THE QUEST FOR TRUE MANHOOOD EXPERIENCE

Welcome to the beginning of an exciting journey: the quest for true manhood! This study is divided into a nine (9) session format plus a bonus summary, each containing the following structure:

THE OVERVIEW: A summary of the chapter content and questions about the topic and focus of the week.

THE PERSONAL QUEST: This includes three (3) segments that you can read, meditate, and respond to during the week. A deeper search for profound meaning and personal growth is possible by probing the referenced scriptures included and reviewing the corresponding chapters in the book What is a Man?

SELF-ASSESMENT: A short series of questions that will allow each man to evaluate his understanding of the topic matter and concept of manhood for that week.

SMALL GROUP SESSIONS: Small group interactive exchange will allow each man to focus on the topic of the week and have the opportunity to share his heart in practical application and testimonies with individuals in their week long study. Small group sessions will involve the gathering with other men, who share their personal observations and insights to encourage one another through the Word of God. Each small group meeting will conclude with a summary of key points, highlights, praise reports and prayer requests.

Recommended Resource(s):
Holy Bible, What is a Man? Book & What is a Man? Workbook.

SESSION I

Understanding: What is a Man?

In this session, the small group will focus upon the following aspects:

- Examine God's original plan and design for man.

- Assess and discuss the cost of living in perpetual immaturity vs. attaining fullness of growth and maturity.

- Distinguish and highlight the critical steps a man must take to fully embrace the high and noble call to manhood.

OVERVIEW

"AND GOD SAID, LET US MAKE MAN IN OUR IMAGE, AFTER OUR LIKENESS..."

GENESIS 1:26

Every man was created to follow the order of his creation, to exist in the "image and likeness of God." Thus, man was destined to serve a high purpose and ultimately fulfill his great & significant calling before God. Man is to reflect God's character: to think, speak, and act in the example of God.

With each step taken away from God's example, image, and likeness, a man only diminishes and subtracts from his manhood. However, those who reconcile themselves to God can begin the wonderful experience of restoration found through God's mercy and grace.

A man can experience great degrees of unspeakable joy when he discovers, embraces, and applies the timeless and priceless truths that allow him to partake of a divine nature that leads him day after day to a wonderful plan as he follows the instructions of God's Word. Only then, will man be the true expression of a great hero and victorious champion that God intended every man to be.

1. Describe in your own words the distorted concept of manhood in today's culture and society?

2. How does today's distorted manhood culture compare and contrast with God's original design and plan as described in Genesis 1:28?

PERSONAL QUEST

SEGMENT 1: REPAIRING TODAY'S DISTORTED VIEW OF MAN

There is no question that the majority of men have lost their way. These disoriented men are distant from and entirely unable to demonstrate the character attributes of genuine manhood and therefore struggle to positively contribute to the other members of their family unit. The poor fruit and lame return on their efforts to familial investments are seen in barren crops. Instead of wholesome families, many men and end up with broken hearts, broken lives, and broken marriages suffering loss and destitute families out of continual failed attempts. Today the men driven by culture find themselves bankrupt and headed for deep destruction, far from God's intended high and noble call for man to be a champion. When man abandons God's creational order for his life, he finds himself falling into disgrace in every area of his life. Instead of dignity, respect, and a place of honor, their life becomes the expression of deviant behavior into a downward spiral toward shame and isolation.

> *"In order to become a great leader, a man must first be willing to become a great follower; and he who refuses to discipline his character has disqualified himself to lead others toward triumph in this life."*

The end result for these men, later in life, is to drown in their sorrows and frustrations into a hellish abyss of addictions, selfishness, and pseudo-intellectualism. Just like the much-celebrated case of the cartoon character Peter Pan, their sole desire is to live out a propetual Neverland experience. Many of these men are totally unable to appropriately respond to reality in the many challenges of true manhood.

"There is a way that seems right to a man and appears straight before him, but at the end of it is the way of death."
Proverbs 14:12

However, when a man decides he will accept the challenge to embrace the high call of manhood and chooses to live a life of obedience, according to the instructions of God's Word, his irresponsibility, rebellion, and childlike fantasies begin to diminish and disappear. During this time, a man can decide to come into serious terms with God, and the hope for maturity becomes a reality. At this time a man begins to flourish and enjoy a great wealth of success, levels of happiness and health he never dreamed possible. He is now able to pursue the path that will allow him to become a great husband, an exemplary father, and an extraordinary world-changing man who makes a great difference wherever he goes.

"The work of righteousness will be peace, and the effect of righteousness, quietness and assurance forever."

Isaiah 32:17

1. What has God prescribed for a man who walks away from His original design? Why do ungodly men suffer agony, confusion, and great depression? (Read Job 20:4-29)

2. According to God's Word, what is the true remedy for the distorted manhood crisis?

3. Read: Deuteronomy 28:13.
What does God promise every man and how can they receive the promise?

SEGMENT 2: GOD'S DESIGN

God designed every man so that they are able to reflect His character. There are no greater expressions of manhood than for men to "think," "talk," and "walk" conveying the image and likeness of God. Therefore, the only true pathway to become a man is to imitate Christ. Paul knew this to be true when he wrote the following Scripture verse.

"And you should imitate me, just as I imitate Christ".
1 Corinthians 11:1

The life of Christ is the ultimate blueprint and model for a man to follow and imitate God. The first steps toward manhood are to willingly imitate Jesus Christ and acknowledge God's divine order as recorded from the beginning of man's creation.

On the very day He created man, God defined and ordained the path men are to follow during their lifetime. In Genesis 1:28, God first blessed man and afterward commanded him to: be fruitful, multiply, fill the earth, subdue it, and take dominion. A man should never forget that from the very start of creation, man's existence, was to conform into God's image and follow the sevenfold creational blessing of manhood. (See. Genesis 1:26 & 28).

> *God desires every man to prosper and to find real lasting significance in all things.*

"… And God blessed man and said to him, be fruitful, multiply, and fill the earth, and subdue it, by using all its vast resources in the service of God and man; and have dominion…"
Genesis 1:28

1. List the manifold attributes of God that man was designed to manifest and reflect?

2. Describe three (3) potential changes that would occur in family and society if a man were to walk in his God-given identity according to the original Biblical pattern of creation.

SEGMENT 3: THE CHALLENGE

God's original intent and desire for every man was to progress, succeed, and continue to live under God's favor and blessing. Thus, man should not allow himself to go astray or come under any curse or embrace any lifestyle contrary to God's design such as sterility, laziness, unfruitfulness, division, emptiness, and selfish diversions or distractions. A man should instead increase in productivity, exercise authority, and take responsibility in the realm of his dominion and within his God-appointed inheritance. In other words, every man should become the champion God created him to be.

> True success is determined by a man's capacity to fulfill the purpose of God during his lifetime.

How can this be possible? First, each man must understand there is a specific sequence to follow in order to fulfill God's wonderful plan to become a champion. This supernatural progression to become a true champion can be compared to the natural progression of plants, which also follow God's creational order and process as follows: (1) a small seed that grows; (2) a plant that blossoms, (3) a flower that produces a fruit, and (4) a fruit that ripens unto maturity.

The following creational order and progression can be seen in God's design for man also, As God's Word declares that God: (1) made man in his own image and likeness, (2) blessed him, (3) commanded him to be fruitful, (4) multiply, (5) fill the earth, (6) subdue the earth, and (7) take dominion on the Earth.

The eternal Creator extends a challenge to every man by commanding him to "listen" and to "obey" God's Word in order to find true purpose and prosperity in their lives. Every man who decides to honor God will receive a position of authority and prominence leading to his enjoyment of great peace and guaranteed prosperity as a result of God's great and faithful reward.

"This Book of my instruction shall not depart from your mouth, but you shall meditate in it day and night, that you may observe to do according to all that is written in it. For then you will make your way very prosperous, and then you will have great success".
Joshua 1:8

As each man repents and returns to follow God's divine order, he will also find the essence of his true identity and be able to fulfill his high and noble call in leading his family to fulfill the divine mandate as prescribed by his Maker, God.

1. Read both: Proverbs 10:22 and Psalm 119:165.
What is the key to a man's true prosperity and great peace?

2. Complete this statement:
God created a man to be:
1-_____
2-_____
3-_____
4-_____
5-_____
6-_____
7-_____

3. In order for a man to re-connect with his God-ordained call to become a true champion, a man needs to:

SELF-ASSESSMENT: After completing the above three (3) segments, each man must take time to evaluate and understand the manhood crisis and God's ordained design for every man.

Be prepared to answer and share some of these answers in the next small group meeting.

1. What are some of the tragic and sad consequences in the home as a result of man's absence, as a husband and/or father?

2. What is the importance in having a good example for learning how to become a true man as God has prescribed in His Word?

3. What does the Word of God say about true success in a man's life?

4. Explain the world changing transformation in Acts 17:6 in the light of God's design and call for every man to lead his generation.

5. How would society's view on manhood change if men would begin to live as God intended men to live from the very beginning?

GROUP MEETING (1 hour):

⌘ **WELCOME & PRAYER** (5 min): Begin by welcoming everyone, introducing each other and asking God to reveal His truth to each man as they begin their journey toward godly manhood.

⌘ **LEADER'S NOTES** (15 min): Leader will share from his notes taken during the first 3 segments and re-read related scripture verse(s) found in What is a Man? Chapter 1- (Gen 1:26,28; 1 Cor. 11:1; Job 20:4-29; Prov. 10:22, 14:12, 16:25; Ps.119:165; Joshua 1:8; Deut. 28:13; Jer. 6:16; Is.32:17).

⌘ **DISCUSSION** (20 min): Each man will be invited to share their notes and begin open dialogue with thoughts concerning the first three (3) segments.

⌘ **ASSESSMENT** (15 min): Leader will read the questions from the "SELF-ASSESMENT" section and invite the men in the small group to share their answers with the rest of the group.

⌘ **PRAYER** (5 min): The meeting will conclude with a prayer asking God that each man capture the vision to return back to God's original creational order to pursue maturity as men designed and created in God's image and likeness to become champions.

SESSION II

JESUS CHRIST THE PERFECT MODEL OF A MAN

In this session, the small group will focus upon the following aspects:

- Identify the facades, disguises, and distractions men use to secretly hide and cover up their lack of manhood.

- Explain the main purpose for Jesus Christ coming to earth.

- Realize that man must follow and imitate Jesus Christ as the perfect model of manhood.

OVERVIEW

"FOR THE SON OF MAN CAME TO SEEK AND TO SAVE THAT WHICH WAS LOST".

LUKE 19:10

No man can find the true meaning and purpose of manhood outside of God. Distant from God, man buys into the lie that the existence of man has origins elsewhere. Others have decided to explain their existence as having come from an ape ancestry and that man's existence upon earth need only a physical component and not a spiritual one. But living for the moment and without God's purpose soon proves to be a meaningless existence causing a man to disguise and cover his deep emptiness with one façade after another. Confusion, foolishness, and darkness are soon to follow. The Bible states, however, that God created man in His own image and provided a design for him to follow after the example of Jesus Christ. When Christ came to earth, his specific purpose was to bring back every man to God's plan. God's provision is perfect and flawless. Only Christ can provide the perfect model to organize a man's thoughts with clarity and give him the certainty to satisfy man's deep longing for purpose, significance, happiness, and obtain the victory that can lead him from "glory to glory."

> *A man's unwillingness to continue in step with Christ renders him lost and totally surrendered to a life without purpose.*

"BUT WE ALL, WITH UNVEILED FACE, BEHOLDING AS IN A MIRROR THE GLORY OF THE LORD, ARE BEING TRANSFORMED INTO THE SAME IMAGE FROM GLORY TO GLORY, JUST AS BY THE SPIRIT OF THE LORD."

2 CORINTHIANS 3:18

PERSONAL QUEST

SEGMENT 1: FACADES, DISGUISES AND DISTRACTIONS

All men desire to become successful and significant. When a man falls short of that reality before others they often times settle for a mere appearance of success. By masquerading self-sufficiency they begin to cover up and reflect an outward façade in every possible way: roaming in the midst of temporal pleasures, indulging in a fantasy world, and creating disguises to seem important and prosperous. For these men the end becomes the same: a perpetual wandering in the dry lands of confusion, uncertainty and emptiness, between one disgraceful veneer to the next.

As seen in the previous session, from the beginning man was created in the image and likeness of God. Therefore, he can only find purpose and understanding for his existence in the light of God's design and call for his life. God desires every man to become successful, prominent and fulfilled. For this reason He sent his Son, Jesus Christ to reconcile man back to God and provide a way for man to return to His original plan to become a champion and a victor.

"I am the way, the truth and the life. No one comes to the Father except through Me."

John 14:6

1. Where does a man most often find his identity or worth?

2. What does the Bible say about a man's identity and worth?

3. Read: 2 Corinthians 3:18.

Explain how a man can live from "glory to glory."

SEGMENT 2: THE PERFECT MODEL

Any man who desires to become a true man must be willing to follow the footsteps of Jesus Christ. Sir Edwin Louis Cole, a respected author and leader of men, states, "Manhood and Christ-likeness are synonymous."

When a man decides to follow and imitate Christ, he begins to take deliberate intentional steps away from child-like selfishness and begins to experience the joy and peace by conforming to the image of Christ. This decision to turn, seek, and begin the pursuit towards maturity and selflessness can lead a man towards the significance and success he seeks in every realm of his life.

In order to ultimately address the issues of modern's man dilemma, better known as, manhood's identity crisis, a man must seek the Lord with his whole heart for Christ alone can offer such salvation and abundant life. As a man draws closer and closer to Jesus, he will find himself enjoying the rightful place, identity, and calling, as a true man in this world. Jesus Christ, among many other things, will:

1. Show him The Way,
2. Give him The Truth,
3. Illuminate his understanding, and
4. Bring him back to a Life full of purpose, significance and meaning.

"The eyes of your understanding being enlightened; that you may know what is the hope of His calling, what are the riches of the glory of His inheritance in the saints..."

Ephesians 1:18

1. Read: Philippians 2:5-11.

Name three (3) attributes of Christ's character that a man can imitate to have a great impact to their life, family, and society in general.

2. Read: Colossians 1:15, 27.

Explain how this principle can help guide a man toward his quest for true manhood.

WHAT IS A MAN? Workbook

SEGMENT 3: THE CHALLENGE

God calls every man to come and find salvation, forgiveness, direction, significance, and prosperity in Jesus Christ. As a man commits to follow Christ's loving words, he can return to God's plan and begin to comprehend each spiritual principle that leads him to a wonderful life. (See. Deut. 28:1-14). In Jesus Christ, God has carefully placed footprints for every man to follow. This challange requires a man to have the courage to come and render accounts before God. Each step will call upon man to accept personal responsibility and show daily fruits of repentance by living in the light of God's Word and instruction.

> **"But you, O man of God, flee these things and pursue righteousness, godliness, faith, love, patience, gentleness."**
> *I Timothy 6:11*

Every man has a daily choice to make. He can continue unwilling, tired, and diminished, totally unable to realize the true significance of his worth by hiding behind facades, disguises, and distractions, which rob man of his true identity and worth. Or alternatively, he can choose to respond to God's Word and march to the trumpet call and challenge that resonates in his heart to attain true manhood by surrendering to God's call.

> **"The thief does not come except to steal, and to kill, and to destroy. I have come that they may have life, and that they may have it more abundantly."**
> *John 10:10*

SELF-ASSESSMENT: After completing the above three (3) segments, take time to evaluate and understand God's purpose for sending Jesus Christ to the earth, as well as the many examples Jesus left for men to follow knowing that "Christ also suffered for us, leaving us an example, that we should follow His steps." (1 Peter 2:21)

Be prepared to share some of these answers in the next small group meeting.

1. Why is it important to study the life of Jesus Christ and imitate him?

2. What does the Bible say about the main purpose for Jesus coming to earth?

3. Explain specific details on how God intended for a man to live and the necessary steps for him to achieve his purpose during his life on earth?

GROUP MEETING (1 hour):

⌘ **WELCOME & PRAYER** (5 min): Begin by welcoming everyone and asking God to place a hunger in each individual to know Christ more intimately and to continue growing in the example of Jesus Christ.

⌘ **LEADER'S NOTES** (15 min): Leader will share from his notes taken during the three (3) segments and re-read the related scripture verse(s) found in What is a Man? Chapter 2 (Luke 19:10, Col. 1:15, 1:27, John14:6, 2Cor. 3:18).

⌘ **DISCUSSION** (20 min): Each man will be invited to share their own notes and begin open dialogue with thoughts concerning the first three (3) segments.

⌘ **ASSESSMENT** (15 min): Leader will read the questions from the "SELF-ASSESMENT" section and invite the men in the small group to share their answers with the rest of the group.

⌘ **PRAYER** (5 min): This meeting will conclude with a final prayer asking God to provide each man with specific situations and opportunities in their daily lives where Jesus Christ can be imitated and His example can be followed.

SESSION III

MAN AS SPIRIT, SOUL, AND BODY

In this session, the small group will focus upon the following aspects:

- Identify the three dimensions of the composition of a man.
- Describe and understand the source of a man's spiritual nourishment.
- Evaluate the results of growing and maturing in man's spirit.

OVERVIEW

"BUT THERE IS A SPIRIT IN MAN: AND IT IS THE BREATH OF GOD ALMIGHTY THAT GIVES HIM UNDERSTANDING".

JOB 32:8

God created every man to be a triune being having a physical body, a soul, and a spirit. God created every man to be a "spirit being," before He gave him a physical body made from the dust of the earth. This aspect of a man's composition, his spirit, allows him to communicate with God. The spirit of man has the capacity to respond to the spiritual realm just as the physical body of man can respond with the five senses. However, due to sin, man's spirit must be revived, awakened, and quickened. The spirit of every man must be nurtured back to life through a new spiritual birth, which begins with a personal relationship through Jesus Christ. As a man recovers his spiritual insight, he can return to fellowship with God and receive the health, wealth, and wisdom to inherit those things prepared for him by God.

"JESUS ANSWERED AND SAID TO HIM, 'MOST ASSUREDELY, I SAY TO YOU, UNLESS ONE IS BORN AGAIN, HE CANNOT SEE THE KINGDOM OF GOD."

JOHN 3:3

After experiencing a new birth, as described in the Gospel of John 3:3, it is of utmost importance for man to nourish his spirit and begin the process towards maturity. The Word of God is the great source of spiritual nourishment for man as the owner's manual to train and develop a man's spirit. As a result of following Jesus as "The Way", man can find the passage way towards "The Truth" which leads to the Father in a measure of existence in a "Life" that cannot otherwise be fulfilled or experienced elsewhere. (See. John 14:6)

1. How can a man's spirit be awakened, made alive, and well nourished?

2. Briefly summarize your coming to Jesus Christ and your spiritual birth experience:

PERSONAL QUEST

SEGMENT 1: THE COMPOSITION OF MAN

> **"For what man knows the things of a man except the spirit of the man which is in him?"**
>
> *1 Corinthians 2:11a*

Man was created by God in the image and likeness of God and composed of three distinct parts: a body, a soul, and a spirit. Men often go through great lengths to take care of their physical body but neglect to adequately nourish their spirit. They often live totally disconnected from God and prefer to wander aimlessly in a life driven by petty priorities and continual selfish decisions. They attempt to hide and cover their emptiness in a desperate deep desire for meaning and significance by highlighting their performance in the intellectual, athletic, financial, and celebrity arenas. Their reality is masked by the glamour of a glossy exterior. Behind the façade, there is a frantic desire and anxiety for true, genuine, and unfading glory.
God created man in his image, since God is spirit; man's essence is also spirit.

This truth is recorded in the earliest of Biblical writings as follows:

> **"But there is a spirit in man: and it is the breath of God Almighty that gives him understanding."**
>
> *Job 32:8*

This is the key to man finding his true meaning and purpose in life: to awaken his spirit to follow God's instructions. How? The spirit must come alive and develop towards getting connected with God's Spirit beginning with a spiritual birth and followed by gradual growth and maturity.

As a man discovers and recovers his spiritual insight, he will begin to walk toward the wealth and inheritance that God has prepared for him

Jesus spoke to a certain man named Nicodemus about being born again (Gospel John 3). This is not a physical birth, but a spiritual birth where every man can begin his journey toward God and becoming the man who would fulfill a great calling and destiny. Ultimately, each man will be defined by the extent and growth of his spirit's maturity.

Paul wrote to the Ephesians church to remind them of the same truth:

"The eyes of your understanding being enlightened; that you may know what is the hope of His calling, what the riches of the glory of His inheritance in the saints."

Ephesians 1:18

1. What does the Bible say about the very essence of man?

2. How can a man's spirit come alive in order to begin to communicate with God and follow His instructions and presence?

3. Why does Jesus Christ teach every man that it is necessary for him to be born again and the great importance there is in nourishing his own spirit?

SEGMENT 2: THE BREAD OF LIFE

To become a true champion it is critical for a man to nourish, train, and govern his own spirit. The nutritional source for such growth is the Holy Bible. This is the Word of God, also known as the bread of life. Obedience to the Word of God becomes the spirit's life source and strength for every man. When Christ overcame Satan's temptations in the wilderness, He showed that true strength to overcome the Devil was found in a spirit nourished in the written provisions of God's Word:

"It is written, 'Man shall not live by bread alone, but by every word that proceeds from the mouth of God."

Matthew 4:4

The prophet Isaiah also reminded men that they should no longer walk in the strength of their own physical body, but by the supernatural gifting of the inner man led by the Spirit of God. Such men are made alive by the Spirit of God and sustained and fortified by the power of His Word.

"There shall come forth a Rod from the stem of Jesse, and a Branch shall grow out of his roots. The Spirit of the Lord shall rest upon Him, the Spirit of wisdom and understanding, the Spirit of counsel and might, the Spirit of knowledge and of the fear of the Lord. His delight is in the fear of the Lord, and He shall not judge by the sight of His eyes, nor decide by the hearing of His ears;"

Isaiah 11:1-3

When a man fails to take personal responsibility to properly nourish his own spirit, it matters little whether it

> Only when a man decides to become accountable for his thoughts, words, and actions, and live by the Word of God, can he find and begin to live God's purpose and plan for his life

is due to his ignorance, neglect, or rebellion. The end result is always the same: suffering, hardship, and great ruin.

Many men prefer finding a refreshing safe haven in the state of fantasy or the perpetual adolescent world of Peter Pan's Never Land. Some end up entangled in drug addiction, alcoholism, pornography, a forbidden relationship of an extra-marital amorous affair, or where reality and responsibility are non-existent.

These men prefer to forego accountability and acceptance of responsibility to become genuine men and rather choose a renegade "born to be wild" lifestyle. But God has a perfect plan to redeem man and help him discover and recover everything he has lost including the vast treasure of purpose and significance in God prepared and laid out for man since the beginning of time. The apostle Paul explains this reality in the following Scripture verse.

"But as it is written: 'Eye has not seen, nor ear heard, nor have entered into the heart of man the things which God has prepared for those who love Him.' But God has revealed them to us through His Spirit. For the Spirit searches all things, yes, and the deep things of God."

1 Corinthians 2:9-10

A man who centers his life in God and lives according to God's plan as described in the Holy Bible can experience the full satisfaction of an unspeakable joy; he will walk toward God's purposes with each step of every day.

1. What is the bread of life? Explain why this is such an appropriate name for God's Word. (See. Matthew 4:4)

2. What is written in Hebrews 11:6 about faith and diligence? Evaluate how much importance a man should dedicate to nourishing his own spirit vs. his physical body? Also, determine what change is required for a man to invest time, effort, and consistency to the Bible so he can become healthy, wealthy, and wise.

SEGMENT 3: SPIRITUAL GROWTH

"He who is slow to anger is better than a mighty warrior, and he who rules his own spirit, than he who captures a city."

Proverbs 16:32

Many say that a man reaches manhood status when he has the capacity to physically care for himself in a responsible manner. In other words, when he can properly physically groom himself and provide for his own sound emotional sustenance. However, these are only two aspects of manhood. Manhood is so much more, namely to encompass man's ability to take on the full responsibility over his whole being: the body, the soul, and the "**spirit**." The hallmark of true manhood includes taking personal responsibility to govern one's own spirit before God, in other words to faithfully care for the essence of one's inner being; the spirit. Manhood therefore, must be measured by a man's ability to live according to God's commandments and one's ability to keep within the parameters of God's instruction.

The Holy Bible prepares man and is able to train him on how to become grounded, rooted, and grown up in all things. The Apostle Peter stated that desiring to know God's word brings about growth like babies who are nourished by milk (1 Pet. 2:2). The author of the Book of Hebrews also reminds every man that the spiritual nutrients found in God's word is able to nourish a man's spirit and will determine the extent of his growth and his development towards maturity (Heb. 5:12-14).

The level of a man's maturity is directly measured by his ability to handle "solid food" and this is determined by the degree to which a man obeys God's instruction. The discipline to receive and live by God's word in every aspect of life should become man's highest priority and pursuit. For example, in the following Scripture verse the Psalmist is able to master his emotions (soul) as a result of a well-nourished spirit in times of anguish and sorrow:

"Why are you cast down, O my soul? And why are you disquieted within me? Hope in God, for I shall yet praise Him for the help of His countenance."

Psalm 42:5

A man's soul is also referred to in the Bible as his "heart." God commands every man to anchor his inner being in faith towards God, rather than to be led astray or shipwrecked by the cares and worries of this life.

"Guard your heart above all else, for it determines the course of your life".

Proverbs 4:23

For this reason, a man must understand the importance of foregoing temporal pleasures of serving "self" in exchange for the pursuit of the eternal attributes of God's character such as righteousness, faith, love, peace, patience, meekness, and excellence. (I Timothy 6:11; Galatians 5:22-23). This becomes the growth track toward maturity. The Bible is clear that those who fail to reach maturity will continue to behave as children and suffer great loss as a result of their irresponsibility (Hebrews 12:14-17). Such men have the tendency to make large promises, but deliver small results. They love to blame others but never take personal ownership for their own actions or inactions; they have children out of wedlock, fail to support their wife and neglect their own children; and sometimes even resort to outbreak of violence, threats and awkward tantrums (Romans 1:21-22). However, those who decide to grow spiritually and reach toward the full stature of maturity can produce good fruit and a harvest by creating a healthy atmosphere for their families, their society, and their world.

"Blessed is the man who trusts in the LORD, and whose hope is the LORD. For he shall be like a tree planted by the waters, which spreads out its roots by the river, and will not fear when heat comes; but its leaf will be green, and will not be anxious in the year of drought, nor will cease from yielding fruit."

Jeremiah 17:7-8

1. Read: Hebrews 5:12-14.

Explain what the Bible means by "milk" vs. "solid food."

2. How can spiritual growth and maturity be measured in a man?

3. List three (3) ways a man can nourish his spirit to overcome temptation and help him obtain victory in his life?

SELF-ASSESSMENT: After completing the above three (3) segments, take time to evaluate your understanding of the true fabric of man's composition and the importance of nourishing the spirit. Make sure each man understands the composition of man's triune being and how each component of a man's being allows him to become a true man.

Be prepared to share some of these answers in the next small group meeting.

1. Why is it important to know and understand that man was created a triune being?

2. What does the Word of God say about the importance of nourishing the body, the soul and the spirit within a man?

3. Describe the character of a man that would be considered a spiritually mature man according to the Bible.

GROUP MEETING (1 hour):

⌘ **WELCOME & PRAYER** (5 min): Begin by welcoming everyone and asking God to reveal himself to every member as they study His word deeper and begin to grow and mature.

⌘ **LEADER'S NOTES** (15 min): Leader will share from his notes taken during the three (3) segments and re-read the related scripture verse(s) found in What is a Man? Chapter 3 (1 Cor. 2:9-11; Job 32:8; Jn.3:3, 14:6, 10:10; Eph.1:18, 4:13; Mt. 4:4; 1 Pet. 2:2; Heb. 5:12-14; 10:5,7; Rom.1:21-22; Is. 11:1-3, Prov. 4:23, 16:32,25:28; Ps. 42:5; I Tim. 6:11;

⌘ **DISCUSSION** (20 min): Each man will be invited to share their own notes and begin open dialogue with thoughts concerning the first three (3) segments.

⌘ **ASSESSMENT** (15 min): Leader will read the questions from the "SELF-ASSESMENT" section and invite the men in the small group to share their answers with the rest of the group.

⌘ **PRAYER** (5 min): This meeting will conclude with a final prayer asking each man to accept responsibility before God to purposefully commit to nourishing his own spirit in greater measure through daily prayer, the studying and obeying of God's Word in order to deliberately connect in fellowship and genuine relationship with God's people at a local church.

SESSION IV

THOUGHTS, WORDS, AND ACTIONS

In this session, the small group will focus upon the following aspects:

- What is the true expression of character in each man?

- Describe and understand the effects and progression of a man's life as his thoughts, words and actions come together to form the road map and blue print for his existence.

- Evaluate how thoughts, words and actions play a part in determining the destiny of a man and how a man's character is formed for better or for worse based on these three aspects of a man's life ever from early childhood.

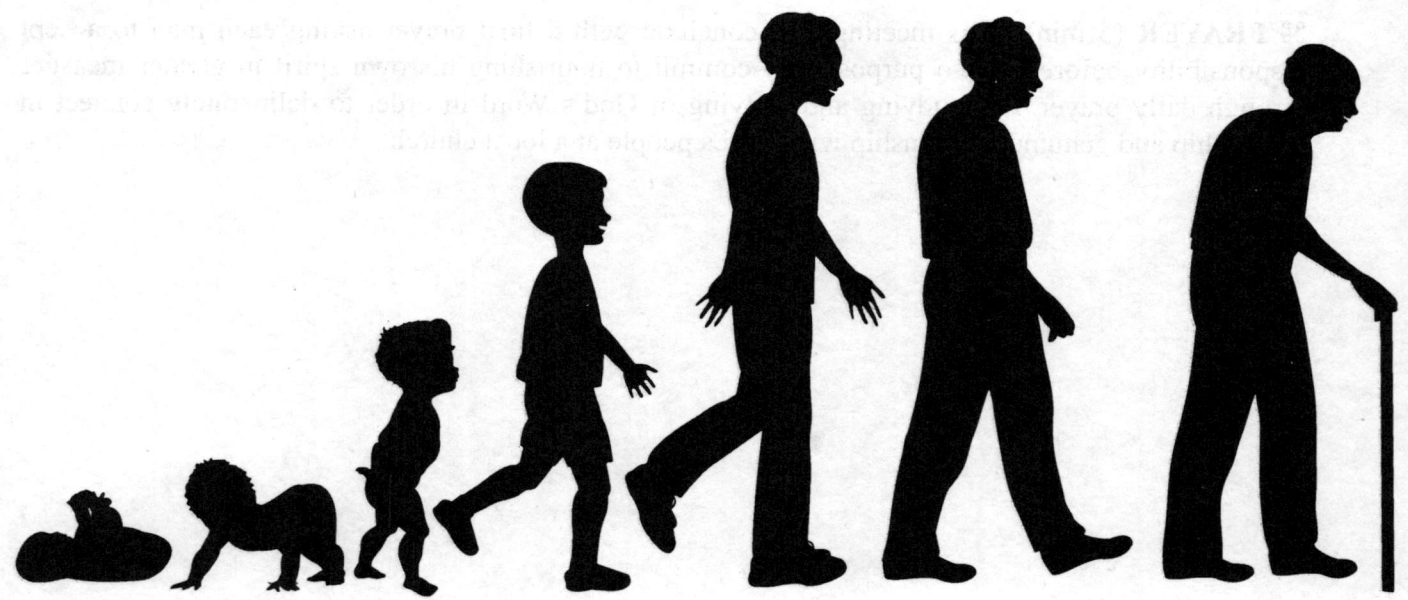

OVERVIEW

"Blessed is the man who walks not in the counsel of the ungodly, nor stands in the path of sinners, nor sits in the seat of the scornful; but his delight is in the law of the lord, and in his law he meditates day and night. He shall be like a tree planted by the rivers of water, that brings forth its fruit in its season, whose leaf also shall not wither; and whatever he does shall prosper."

Psalm 1:1-3

Thoughts are a weighty matter. What a man thinks can spark his conscience and lead him to a marvelous future or toward a downward spiral of destruction. A man's thought life initiates the process of formulating words, and subsequently, forming his actions. Suitable thoughts will lead to proper words, which in turn can catapult a man toward a bright future. The opposite is true, bad thoughts can lead a man and his words to destroy like gangrene and diminish a man to an inferno of horrible acts in wicked proportions.

> *Man's thoughts will determine his words and actions, which in turn will establish his habits, forge his character, and decide his destiny.*

The well-trained thoughts and pleasant words of a man are a continual source of direction for fitting conduct. All of man's deeds reflect one of two realities: the glory inherited by a wise man or the shame inherited by the fool. Those who challenge the prescribed order of God will suddenly endure hardships and come into a ruin they wish they had never to have tasted.

"The human pride will be humbled, and human arrogance will be brought down. Only the Lord will be exalted on that Day of Judgment. Idols will completely disappear."

Isaiah 2:17-18

Encouraging a man to ***think*** differently allows him to begin to ***live*** differently. The essence of a man's thought life should therefore be directed toward those things prescribed by God's word. As a man meditates in honorable, organized, and well-grounded thoughts, his life begins to reflect the same. A passage from the Bible found in the book of Philippians serves as an excellent example to filter a man's thoughts and also provides a healthy description and safe boundaries for his thought life,:

"Finally, brethren, whatever things are true, whatever things are noble, whatever things are just, whatever things are pure, whatever things are lovely, whatever things are of good report, if there is any virtue and if there is anything praiseworthy—meditate on these things."

Philippians 4:8

1. Why can thoughts become the determining factor in a man's life and final destiny?

2. How can the mere words of a man catapult him toward greatness or plunge him into horrible destruction?

3. Explain Proverbs 23:7 in the context of this session.

PERSONAL QUEST

SEGMENT 1: SUITABLE THOUGHTS

The many single tiny grains of sand that have accumulated on the shores over a great period of time form the coastlines of every nation. Likewise, a man's character is formed by the sum total of many thoughts, words, and actions accumulated over a lifetime. A man's entire existence is formed by the thoughts that he has allowed to occupy his daily meditation. If a man's thoughts are dedicated to God and kept upon God's Word, then his identity will be founded upon God's truth and purpose. Otherwise, he will attract a myriad of unrealistic, blatantly infantile thoughts that would lead him toward destructive desires. For this reason, Biblical teaching warns and forbids man from making or serving any false or graven images:

"...do not make for yourselves any false image in the form of anything, the Lord your God has forbidden this."

Deuteronomy. 4:23

The intensity of a man's wrongful meditation and the depth of his evil thoughts can predict the downfall of a man. To the contrary, the faithful training of wholesome meditation propels the rise and great prosperity of another man whose thoughts are kept upon God's Word and the resulting aligning of his words and actions to God's counsel. A man's thoughts stayed upon God's Word will lead him to God's plan.

"And do not be conformed to this world, but be transformed by the renewing of your mind, that you may prove what is that good and acceptable and perfect will of God."

Romans 12:2

Every man must discipline his mind to be conformed to the obedience and submission of Christ. Its importance cannot be overstated; it is like the black box of an aircraft. From time to time, federal investigators seek to find the cause of an airplane's tragic crash. They first seek to locate the black box, the electronic device that records what happened right before the accident and what factors might have contributed to the plane's disastrous end. Likewise, the thoughts of a man many times lead him to speak words and take actions that are contrary to his best interest. Allowing the Spirit of God to fill our mind with godly thoughts can result in wholesome, productive, and healthy words. Finally, these words become the seeds that bring a harvest of blessings, peace, and fruitfulness in a man's conduct toward a blessed life.

> *"Casting down arguments and every high thing that exalts itself against the knowledge of God, bringing every thought into captivity to the obedience of Christ..."*
>
> **2 Corinthians 10:5**

1. How can a man exercise dominion over his thought life? Summarize two passages in the Bible that are helpful in this area.

2. Distinguish between the inner "renewal of the mind" and outer "transformation" as described by the Apostle Paul in Romans 12:2

3. Commit the verse in Philippians 4:8 to memory and write it down in the space provided:

4. As per Psalm 1:2-3, what are the benefits of thinking and meditating upon God's Word day and night rather than following the counsel of the ungodly and sinner?

SEGMENT 2: PROPER WORDS

"May these words of my mouth and this meditation of my heart be pleasing in your sight, Lord, my Rock and my Redeemer".

Psalm. 19:14

Words are a powerful force for a man that when properly constructed can build him a bridge to a wonderful future or when misplaced can result in casting him over a cliff into a dark, depraved course, of regrettable consequences. Carelessness in a man's thoughts tends to breed carelessness in his words. The Bible states that a man's words are spoken from the abundance of his heart. (See. Matthew 12:34-37) This truth has been repeatedly proven throughout man's history. The words uttered or spoken over a man ultimately become the driving force of his future and reality.

Learning to speak words with precision and accuracy can be compared to navigating a vessel toward a safe harbor. A competent captain carefully takes the helm of ship and skillfully steers the rudder to move his large vessel away from strong windstorms and danger. Likewise, a wise man demonstrates self-control through the careful use of his words:

"If any man offend not in word, the same is a perfect man, and able to restrain his whole body"

James 3:2

The following verses help a man to use his words wisely:

1. Speak with restraint; not rashly (Proverbs 13:3)
2. Speak with maturity; not childishly (2 Timothy 2:16-18)
3. Speak with humility; not arrogantly (Isaiah 2:17-18; Proverbs 16:18)
4. Speak with eternity in mind; not carelessly (Proverbs 1:31)

Finally, the apostle Paul warns his young apprentice Timothy that a man should guard his own lips and avoid gathering with those who enjoy the exercise of godless chatter because this leads more and more toward diminishing of manly character.

"Avoid godless chatter, because those who indulge in it will become more and more ungodly [the opposite of true manhood]. Their teaching will spread like gangrene. Among them are Hymenaeus and Philetus, who have departed from the truth [reality]...."

2 Timothy 2:16-18

1. Read: James 3:1-12.

Explain at length the parallel between a <u>rudder, a horse bit,</u> and <u>a spark</u> that starts a forest fire in relation to a man's tongue.

2. What results would come to a family, church, and society if all men decided to speak with proper words with the caution and careful understanding that words have the power to bless or curse?

3. If a man's life becomes the image and reality of the words he has spoken, what wise, wholesome, productive, and wonderful words would he begin to utter?

4. Which specific words should a man eliminate from his vocabulary to avoid seeing destruction in his lifetime?

SEGMENT 3: NOBLE ACTIONS

"Be not deceived; evil conversations corrupt good character."
1 Corinthians 15:33

The combination of thoughts and words a man embraces mark him for life because these are eventually embodied in his express overt acts and conduct. These acts over time determine regular habits that forge the character of a man. And finally, a man's character dictates his future end.

Strength of character begins in the mind and is reflected in the words and actions of man. God designed a process whereby man, through the renewal of his mind, is able to experience real transformation. This renewal process begins with the washing of a man's mind through God's Word and an honest pursuit to conform to God's order and design in all things.

Every man has a clear choice, he may think, speak, and live haphazardly or submit his members as orderly instruments of righteousness to fulfill God's high call towards excellence. When a man chooses to live carelessly or reckless, his world becomes a whirlwind of total destruction and confusion. Men, who live with a casual approach, paying little attention to their thoughts and words, will experience life in a series of meaningless events, irrational circumstances, and unrelated chapters. The greatest tragedy is that they will continue to suffer disconnectedness from reality from one generation to another.

However, when a man chooses to set his pride to one side and makes God's plan his priority, he becomes qualified to participate in every good work prepared for him by God and ultimately find a genuine acceptance in securing a blessed future.

"The work of righteousness will be peace, and the effect of righteousness, quietness and assurance forever. My people will dwell in a peaceful habitation, in secure dwellings, and in quiet resting places..."

Isaiah 32:17-18

1. List five (5) "good works" prepared for a man willing to walk according to God's will as described in Ephesians 2:10.

   a-_____

   b-_____

   c-_____

   d-_____

   e-_____

2. Explain two (2) areas that a man is most vulnerable to be attacked by the enemy and provide two (2) verses of Scripture as references.

3. Summarize the sequence of events that follow in a man's life from the conception of a thought to his final destiny.

SELF-ASSESSMENT: After completing the above three (3) segments, take time to consider, evaluate, and understand the impact of a man's thoughts, words, and actions in relation to his life, family, church, work, and community.

Be prepared to share some of these answers in the next small group meeting.

1. Why is it important for a man to place value and significance upon his thought life and meditation?

2. Read- James 3:1-11
What does the Bible say about the power of the tongue and a man's spoken words?

3. Describe the end of a man who has cultivated a healthy thought life and who chooses to be careful to guard his lips.

GROUP MEETING (1 hour):

⌘ **WELCOME & PRAYER** (5 min): Begin by welcoming everyone and pray to God asking Him to renew every man's thoughts and minds so that they learn to speak the correct words and experience true transformation and lasting fulfillment.

⌘ **LEADER'S NOTES** (15 min): Leader will share from his notes taken during the three (3) segments and re-read the related scripture verse(s) found in What is a Man? Chapter 4 (1 Cor. 15:33; Ps. 1:1-3; Rom 12:2; Phil. 4:8; Prov. 1:31, 13:3, 16:18, 21:23, 23:7; Deut. 4:23; Prov. 18:21; James 3:2; 2 Tim. 2:16-18;. 1:31; Is. 2:17-18).

⌘ **DISCUSSION** (20 min): Each man will be invited to share their own notes and begin open dialogue with thoughts concerning the first 3 segments.

⌘ **ASSESSMENT** (15 min): Leader will read the questions from the "SELF-ASSESMENT" section and invite the men in the small group to share their answers with the rest of the group.

⌘ **PRAYER** (5 min): The meeting will conclude with a final prayer asking God that each man become a true leader in his generation and over his family; beginning to cultivate a pure thought life, speech and conduct that honors God.

SESSION V

TIME, TALENTS, AND TREASURES

In this session, the small group will focus upon the following aspects:

- What is God's priority for a man regarding his time, talents, and treasures as opposed to the popular worldly culture's priority.

- Reflect on how a man's time, talents, and treasure can be directed for God's Glory in contrast to man's glory.

- Create a new personal plan of investment for man in these three areas that reflect a new understanding for the godly stewardship of time, talents and treasures.

OVERVIEW

This is what the Lord says:
"Let not the wise boast of their wisdom or the strong boast of their strength or the rich boast of their riches, but let the one who boasts boast about this: that they have the understanding to know me, that I am the Lord, who exercises kindness, justice and righteousness on earth, for in these I delight," declares the Lord."

Jeremiah 9:23-24

Every man has been entrusted with a specific measure of time, talents, and treasures from God. After aligning his triune being (body, soul, and spirit) and his thoughts, words, and actions to the counsel of God; a man must also review his understanding of godly stewardship.

The first step is to acknowledge his need for wisdom and divine instruction. Secondly, a man must realize and appreciate the urgency of using these three amazing gifts for God's eternal purposes because his time on earth is limited and material treasures can suffer waste after time.

Count your days and navigate life with purposeful intent.

"And He has made from one blood every nation of men to dwell on all the face of the earth, and has determined their pre-appointed times and boundaries of their dwellings..."

Acts 17:26

Some men seem to forget that their days are numbered upon the earth. A wise man cherishes his life as a gift from God and seeks to earnestly fulfill every task according to God's plan and timetable. Accordingly, each man is called by God to serve his Creator as well as others with his talents and resources. The wise and proper uses of a man's time, talents, and treasures will not only ultimately determine his rewards in eternity but also during his dwelling here upon the earth.

"Do not lay up for yourselves treasures on earth, where moth and rust destroy and where thieves break in and steal; but lay up for yourselves treasures in heaven, where neither moth nor rust destroys and where thieves do not break in and steal. For where your treasure is, there your heart will be also."
Matthew 6:19-21

1. How often does a man think about eternity? Why is that?

2. Read: Matthew 6:33
Explain whether the following statement is correct or incorrect and why?

"A man's earthly existence requires him to concern himself **most** with his time, talents, and treasure focused upon his earthly needs."

PERSONAL QUEST

SEGMENT 1: THE VALUE OF TIME

"So teach us to number our days, that we may gain a heart of wisdom."

Psalm 90:12

When a man is able to properly manage his time, talents, and treasures, he excels and prospers in all things. Every man must realize that time is a valuable asset but limited. God has allotted a portion of time as a gift to every man and this must be used very wisely. A man is to use his time to discover and develop the talents God has bestowed upon him so he can fulfill God's great call.

A faithful man grows in his ability to perfect his schedule and always seeks to honor God with his time. This man also understands and values other people's time. Many men squander their days, failing to see the importance and value of time, but later wish they could turn back the clock and redeem the wasted time, but this becomes impossible. For this reason, a man must discern the times and the seasons to diligently work to fulfill God's purpose.

"To everything there is a season, a time for every purpose under heaven."

Ecclesiastes 3:1

God has given every man a measure of time to fulfill a great purpose. During this shortly allotted time, a man must learn to refine and sharpen his character. This takes an expression of growing in different aspects of his earthly existence, but most importantly attaining the measure, stature and fullness of Christ-likeness. Therefore, time is of the essence and learning to live each minute with eternity in mind will prove beneficial and rewarding for man.

1. Read 1Chronicles 12:32.
Explain what is meant by the phrase "understanding of the times."

2. Ask God in prayer to reveal the proper order and importance of time and how a man should discover priorities for the season he is in; then purpose to diligently make the necessary changes to live accordingly.

SEGMENT 2: UNIQUE TALENT

"See thou a man diligent in his business? He shall stand before kings; he shall not stand before unknown men."

Proverbs 22:29

God has gifted every man with a different measure of talent that is exclusive and unique to each man. These talents are small expressions of God's unparalleled and exceptional characteristics. Distinct and special talents were given to each man so that he may uniquely serve God and benefit others.

The proper use of a man's time, talents, and treasure will ultimate determined his rewards.

Man's correct response in the light of these talents is to identify and develop them to the highest possible degree for the glory of God. For example, if a man can jump, then he must jump to the highest level; if his talent is running, then he must run as fast as humanly possible. The discovery, training, and highest use of these talents for God is a genuine form of worship.

The opposite is true. If a man mismanages his time and talents, he will only find emptiness and lack of satisfaction as described in the ancient book of Ecclesiastes:

"Therefore I hated life; because the work that is wrought under the sun is grievous unto me: for all is vanity and vexation of spirit."

Ecclesiastes 2:17

Here, King Solomon expresses himself as a man whose heart is disconnected from God in times and seasons. As a result, he hated life, suffered great loss, and wasted his talents and treasures on meaningless vanity. The purpose for this Old Testament account is so that a man might not pursue the same futility of thought. Instead, a man should discern the times, develop his talents, and serve God and his generation with excellence in God's purpose and treasure.

"The hand of the diligent shall bear rule: but the slothful shall be under tribute."

Proverbs 12:24

1. List the first five (5) of your talents that come to mind:

    a- _____
    b- _____
    c- _____
    d- _____
    e- _____

2. How true is this statement (Explain your answer):
   I am using my best efforts with all my God given talents to diligently serve God and others.

3. How would the following advice help a man to better steward his time, talents and treasures?

"Hey Sir, pray to God that you can clear up the clutter to free more time on your daily calendar to develop the under-used talents, overcome timidity to live by faith instead of fear, be more consistent to utilize your treasures to invest in the kingdom of God and increase your eternal portfolio in heaven's priority by serving Jesus Christ and His church where there is an open opportunity and the need is real."

SEGMENT 3: ETERNAL TREASURE

"But seek first the kingdom of God and His righteousness, and all these things shall be added to you."

Matthew 6:33

There is no doubt, that a man who has been diligent with his time and talent can accumulate great treasure by the end of his life. However, these men would have to ask themselves what was their driving force and motive during this time. Jesus declared long ago that life is more than possessions and knowing God greater than gaining the whole world:

"And he said unto them, Take heed, and beware of covetousness; for a man's life does not consist in the abundance of things which he possesses."

Luke 12:15

"For what will it profit a man if he gains the whole world, and loses his soul?"

Mark 8:36

The achievement of greatness in wisdom, power in might, and vast riches is only significant in the light of understanding God's purpose for man. Man was not created to simply plow through life from one hardship to the next, void of any true meaning or significance. Rather, God designed man to intimately communicate with His Creator and to enjoy a personal relationship with Him. Only then can man experience God's eternal love and fulfill His eternal purpose.

In conclusion, the secret of true manhood is this: for man to grow, mature, and consistently live synchronized with God's heart and joined to His purpose in each of the nine expressions of a man's earthly existence:

- ▶ **Body, soul, and spirit**
- ▶ **Thoughts, words, and actions**
- ▶ **Time, talents, and treasures**

The result will be a man that can bless his family, impact his community, and change the world.

1. What is the meaning behind Jesus words that it is better for a man to accumulate treasures in heaven? **See.** Matthew 6:19-21

2. Is having great wealth upon this earth a sin? Why or why not?

3. What can a man begin to do in his local church to influence his family and community in regards to living within God's eternal purpose?

SELF-ASSESSMENT: After completing the above three (3) segments, take time to consider, evaluate, and understand the impact of one man's legacy to his family, church and community as a result of properly using and stewarding his time, talents, and treasures according to God's divine plan.

Be prepared to share some of these answers in the next small group meeting.

1. Explain "godly stewardship" for a man who is totally surrendered to God.

2. What is the proper balance for a man and how he should steward his time, talents and treasures at home, work, and ministry? Explain.

3. Give three (3) examples of how a man can lay up treasures in heaven.

a- _____

b- _____

c- _____

GROUP MEETING (1 hour):

⌘ **WELCOME & PRAYER** (5 min): Begin by welcoming everyone and pray asking God for each man to become a better steward of his time, talents, and treasures, so that his influence is not diminished but increased as a man who lives each day for the glory of God.

⌘ **LEADER'S NOTES** (15 min): Leader will share from his notes taken during the three (3) segments and re-read the related scripture verse(s) found in What is a Man? Chapter 5 (Acts 17:26; Ps. 90:12; Ecc. 2:17, 3:1; 1 Chron. 12:32; Prov. 12:24, 22:29; Luke 12:15; Mk. 8:36; Mt. 6:19-21,33; Jer. 9:23-24).

⌘ **DISCUSSION** (20 min): Each man will be invited to share their own notes and begin open dialogue with thoughts concerning the first three (3) segments.

⌘ **ASSESSMENT** (15 min): Leader will read the questions from the "SELF-ASSESMENT" section and invite the men in the small group to share their answers with the rest of the group.

⌘ **PRAYER** (5 min): The meeting will conclude with a prayer asking God to give each man the wisdom and diligence to wisely invest his time, talents, and treasures according to God's prescribed schedule and plan.

SESSION VI

FAITHFULNESS: THE CORNERSTONE OF CHARACTER

In this session, the small group will focus upon the following aspects:

- Understanding the distinctions between a child and a mature man.

- Determine the measurable characteristics of a faithful man.

- What are the correlations between responsibility and maturity?

OVERVIEW

"When I consider Your heavens, the work of Your fingers, the moon and the stars, which You have ordained, what is man that You are mindful of him, and the son of man that You visit him? For You have made him a little lower than the angels, and You have crowned him with glory and honor. You have made him to have dominion over the works of Your hands; You have put all things under his feet."

Psalm 8:3-6

Men who are faithful and responsible seem to be a species of man close to total extinction. In today's culture there is a serious social phenomenon, an unusual trend toward grave consequences: men are refusing to grow up. When this astonishing condition occurs to a man it has become our preference to classify this behavior as the "Peter Pan Syndrome." Anytime a man refuses to grow up and decides to perpetuate and prolong his adolescence, everyone in his social sphere suffers: marriages, families, society, and the world as a whole. Immature men refuse to take responsibility choosing rather to display a demeanor or poise that is unstable, erratic, inconsistent, and unreliable. These men arrogantly proclaim to be filled with greatness, but end up with the final delivery of poor performance and a tract record of worthless accomplishments.

Know that the Lord, He is God; it is He who has made us and not we ourselves; we are His people and the sheep of His pasture".

Psalm 100:3

God is very interested in developing every man's character. Since the beginning of time, God's desire was to see man prosper and flourish. The character of a man reveals his inner spirit. The best way to test a man's character is to allow him to experience pressure in the midst of adversity. A man's ability to properly respond on a consistent basis during times of hardship and difficulty can prove his noble character.

> **"If you faint in the day of adversity, your strength is small."**
> **Proverbs 24:10**

1. Why is faithfulness necessary to fulfill God's calling for man?

2. What impact does responsibility have in a man's life, marriage, family, church, and community?

3. What is a man's "perfected character" from the Bible's viewpoint?

PERSONAL QUEST

SEGMENT 1: FAITHFULNESS

"Most men will proclaim his own goodness, but who can find a faithful man?"

Proverbs 20:6

From the very beginning God created man to entrust him with the awesome responsibility to steward all His works. The Bible reveals that all things upon earth were placed under man's dominion so that he might rule and govern over them as God's appointed representative. From the inception of creation God positioned man to have authority by "crowing him with glory and honor" (Hebrews 2:7). For this reason, it is necessary that every man become truly faithful so that he is able to carry the weight of glory and responsibility entrusted to him by God.

"My eyes shall be on the faithful of the land, that they may dwell with me; he who walks in a perfect way, he shall serve me".

Psalm 101:6

Faithfulness is the cornerstone of the true masculine character. A faithful man will display: determination, strength of character, stability, conviction, courage, loyalty, and integrity despite the adverse circumstances. On the other hand, an unfaithful man resembles the character of Satan by continually exhibiting confusion, chaos, abandonment, betrayal, hatred, instability, and disloyalty among many things. Such a man cannot be entrusted with God's precious treasure for he will exhibit his lack of manhood by causing others to suffer much pain.

"Placing confidence in an unfaithful man in time of trouble is like a bad tooth and a foot out of joint."

Proverbs 25:19

1. Why is faithfulness necessary to fulfill God's calling as a man?

2. Compare and contrast some of the reactions of a faithful man vs. an unreliable man:

3. What impact does responsibility have in a man's life, marriage, family, church, and community?

4. What is a man's "perfected character" from the Bible's viewpoint?

5. Based on this chapter, what words describe a "faithful man" at home, church, and the community at large?

SEGMENT 2: THE CALAMITY OF AN UNFAITHFUL MAN

"But the wicked will be cut off from the land and the unfaithful will be uprooted from it."

Proverbs 2:22

Travel anywhere upon the earth today and one will find an alarming lack of faithful men. Every ruin upon the earth can be traced back to an unfaithful man. The earth has been sadly populated with a landscape of unfaithful men who abandon their call to faithfulness. Wherever one looks in the present generation the calamity of unfaithful men are evident. Unwanted pregnancy, divorce, abortions, high crime rates, scandal, devastation, political unrest, terrorism, and governmental misappropriation are all the results of an unfaithful man.

"Thus I will make the land desolate, because they have acted unfaithfully,' declares the Lord GOD."

Ezekiel 15:8

Just as faithfulness is the cornerstone of a man's true character, unfaithfulness is the calamity of all peoples in family, at church, in community, and nations. An unfaithful man will display: cowardness, weakness of character, instability, spineless existence, resistance to order, treachery, infidelity, compromise and becomes the catalyst to a degenerate existence. Taking on the character attributes of Satan himself, an unfaithful man becomes blight to his family, church, and community by leaving behind an atmosphere of confusion, unfruitful, uncertainty, and selfish chaos. Such a man seems to walk and exist only to plunder the abundance of God's vast provision by his selfish, self-centered, and sinister character.

"The thief does not come except to steal, and to kill, and to destroy. I have come that they may have life, and that they may have it more abundantly."

John 10:10

Truthfully, an unfaithful man is unwelcomed in any social circle. These weak willed men are despised by women, resented by their children and rejected by society as a whole because they profess to love, enter into commitments and profess authenticity but are truly unable to deliver any of these realities. The appearance of an unfaithful man is able to sell his personality but cannot deliver true substance because of his ungodly character. The unfaithful man is quick to proclaim the strength of his character, the depth of his moral conviction and sincerity of his thoughts and intentions until a wave of adversity rises up, where he will abandon ship revealing the true lack of his integrity. An unfaithful man is without character, unable to offer himself to serve others and incapable of serving God and as a result of his selfishness will disintegrate and suffer a horrendous falling out beyond repair. The unfaithful man does not benefit from any correction, wisdom or instruction and therefore is headed to great calamity and destruction without remedy. God is willing to walk with a faithful man a thousand miles but He draws a serious line to never take one step with the unfaithful man.

"The integrity of a faithful man will guide him, but the perversity of the unfaithful will destroy them."

Proverbs 11:3

"He who is often rebuked, and hardens his neck, will suddenly be destroyed, and that without remedy."

Proverbs 29:1

1. Why is the earth filled with so many calamities?

2. List five (5) tragic calamities that are direct consequences of an unfaithful man.

a-_____
b-_____
c-_____
d-_____
e-_____

3. Read James 1:27.
Who are the most affected or impacted by an unfaithful man?

4. What curses come upon an unfaithful man at home, church, and the community at large?

SEGMENT 3: STEADFAST VS. ERRATIC

There are a few things more painful than a toothache or a broken foot. These illustrations describe the experience of those who have suffered the aftermath and dealings of an unfaithful man: long term scars, feelings of ruin and despair, trail of tears, including broken hearts, broken dreams, broken homes, and broken lives.

Many men boast about their faithfulness and allegiance. They are quick to proclaim strength of character, depth of moral conviction, and sincerity of thoughts, words, and actions. However, when a wave of adversity rises, the truth about their integrity and steadfastness is revealed. Instead of following after the image and likeness of God, they are blinded by hell's most sinister being: Satan. Thus, they display erratic decision-making, continual changes in jobs, relationships, and other responsibilities. They lack the healthy expressions of appropriate behavior belonging to a mature adult. As a result, such men lose the hope of the desired goal and the promised expectation of future rewards.

"But even if our gospel is veiled, it is veiled to those who are perishing, whose minds the god of this age has blinded, who do not believe, lest the light of the gospel of the glory of Christ, who is the image of God, should shine on them."

2 Corinthians 4:3-4

What is the remedy to this desperate devastation? A man willing to seek after God and draw near to Him with relentless sincerity and undaunted surrender can change the course of this calamity. A man who is willing to search, seek, and find his restoration, renewal, and reconciliation with God. As a man grows to become more and more like Christ, he will demonstrate a character that does not forsake nor abandon those he has professed and called to love, keep and care for. This captures and explains the great mystery of how God desires to seek man and restore him with glory and honor. Rather than man being tossed to and fro like a tumbleweed in the wilderness, God's plan for man is to plant him and allow him to take deep roots in order to yield much fruit to glorify God during his time upon the earth.

> **"That we should no longer be children, tossed to and fro and carried about with every wind of doctrine."**
>
> **Ephesians 4:14**

1. List five (5) childish reactions men often display and the five (5) ways mature man should respond to avoid immature outburst.

Immature	Mature
a- _____	a- _____
b- _____	b- _____
c- _____	c- _____
d- _____	d- _____
e- _____	e- _____

2. What character-type of man does God, bless, reward, and prosper?

3. How can a man re-connect with God to reflect the glory of his original design?

4. What is steadfastness?

5. Read Psalm 8:3-6.
What is the purpose of man's God-given authority?

SELF-ASSESSMENT

In the following passages, Explain the manner is which God deals with unfaithful man.

1. 1 John 1:9 _____

2. Philippians 1:6 _____

3. Ezekiel 36:27 _____

Be prepared to share some of these answers in the next small group meeting.

GROUP MEETING (1 hour):

⌘**WELCOME & PRAYER** (5 min): Begin by welcoming everyone and open in prayer asking the Holy Spirit that the faithfulness expressed by God's character become the reality manifested by the men to their spouse, children, family and church and that unfaithful men would repent asking for forgiveness where they have been unfaithful.

⌘**LEADER'S NOTES** (15 min): Leader will share from his notes taken during the three (3) segments and re-read the related scripture verse(s) found in What is a Man? Chapter 6 (Prov. 20:6, 24:10, 25:19; Psalms 8:3-6, 100:3, 101:6 including workbook Scripture verse(s) Proverbs 2:22, Ezekiel 15:8, John 10:10, Proverbs 11:3, Proverbs 29:1)

⌘**DISCUSSION** (20 min): Each man will be invited to share their own notes and begin open dialogue with thoughts concerning the first three (3) segments.

⌘**ASSESSMENT** (15 min): Leader will read the questions from the "SELF-ASSESMENT" section and invite the men in the small group to share their answers with the rest of the group.

⌘**PRAYER** (5 min): The meeting will conclude with prayer asking God to grant each man the gift and opportunity to repent from their unfaithfulness and ask God to perfect and allow them to flourish in their faithfulness to follow Christ as their example in every area of their life according to Hebrews 3:5-6.

SESSION VII

GODLY MAN OR PETER PAN

In this session, the small group will focus upon the following aspects:

- Identify childlike behaviors and consequences.

- Understand the key to successful marriages and parenting.

- Outline the prerequisites for exercising authority according to the Biblical model.

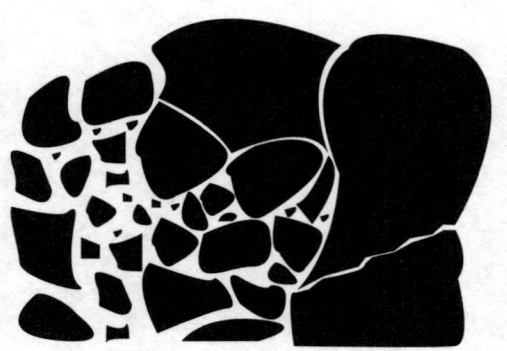

OVERVIEW

Much like the fictional Disney caricature known as Peter Pan, many men avoid reality and prefer to live absent of responsibility in a fanciful mindset, in a make-believe place called Never Land. However, the fantasy comes to an abrupt end when these men suddenly face the haunting consequences of their irresponsibility.

Anytime a man refuses to grow up and decides to perpetuate and prolong his adolescence, everyone loses: marriages, families, the work place, society, and the world as a whole. Immature men refuse to take responsibility choosing rather to display a demeanor and poise that is unstable, erratic, inconsistent, and unreliable. These men arrogantly proclaim to be filled with greatness, but end up with the final poor delivery and performance accumulating a continued tract record of worthless and incomplete accomplishments. This phenomena was described by Jesus Christ when He declared the following Scripture verse.

"But to what shall I liken this generation? It is like children sitting in the marketplace and calling to their companions."
Matthew 11:16

In the Old Testament Book of 1 Kings, the Bible records the story of a man named Adonijah, the son of King David, who attempted to live in his fantasy world. He exalted himself in rebellion against his father's rule and made plans to overthrow his father's throne. But his intention to violently usurp his father's kingdom, abruptly ended when he died a tragic and shameful death. The Scriptures record that this man was never held accountable by his father David, who failed to confront and discipline his son. As a result, Adonijah was never able to face the consequences of his actions until it was too late.

"Then Adonijah the son of Haggith exalted himself, saying, "I will be king"; and he prepared for himself chariots and horsemen, and fifty men to run before him. (And his father had not rebuked him at any time by saying, "Why have you done so?" He was also very good-looking. His mother had borne him after Absalom)."

1 Kings 1:5-6

In his biblical letters, the Apostle Paul points out that the most important step in becoming a true man is having the willingness to face reality and abandon childlike fantasy. A mature man must think, speak, and act in unison of character. God requires every man to first govern his own spirit, before attempting to be held accountable for others, such as his wife, children, and ministry. When a man is born again in Christ, God gives him the rights and inheritance of a firstborn for the purpose of reaching maturity, imparting this inheritance to others, and passing it down to the following generation.

1. When men refuse to mature or take responsibility, what are the results to a marriage, family, business, and community?

2. According to I Kings 1:5-6, what are the consequences of a man not being held accountable by his father for his thoughts, words, and actions?

3. What words best describe a mature man?

4. Read Romans 14:12 and 1 Corinthians 3:12-15)
   What does the Bible say about being accountable as a man?

PERSONAL QUEST

SEGMENT 1: GROWING UP

Manhood is reached through the process of slowly progressing from child-like behavior until shwoing forth full maturity. In good or bad times, a mature man will live by choosing careful words, thinking rightful thoughts, and acting with deliberate wisdom, responsibility, and faithfulness. He will show the true measure of the character of Christ in all things and at all times. To the contrary, an immature man will perpetuate a child-like mentality by speaking improperly, contemplate stagnate thinking, and engage in behaviors contrary to maturity as God has planned for his life.

"When I was a child, I spoke as a child, I understood as a child, I thought as a child, but when I became a man I left behind my childish ways."

I Corinthians 13:11

The journey from childhood to manhood begins when a man becomes responsible for himself and stops making excuses for not governing his own spirit. The Bible compares a man who fails to govern his own spirit to a city with broken walls: unprotected and without provision or purpose. Although they may find some semblance of success in particular areas of their lives, they neglect the most important aspect, namely; their spirit. As a result, everything these men have will be taken away violently, not by God, but as a consequence of their own personal irresponsibility and childish ways.

"Whoever has no rule over his own spirit is like a city broken down, without walls."

Proverbs 25:28

1. According to 1 Corinthians 13:11, what three (3) specific areas in a man must change before true maturity can occur?

   a._____
   b._____
   c._____

2. What are five (5) ways a man can govern his own spirit?

   a._____
   b._____
   c._____
   d._____
   e._____

3. Name three (3) spiritual treasures God has entrusted upon every man so that he may pass onto the next generation.

   a._____
   b._____
   c._____

4. Who is responsible for passing a legacy of blessing to the next generation?

SEGMENT 2: MANHOOD: FROM GROOM TO FATHERHOOD

A man who can govern his own spirit can be entrusted with the care and the nourishment of the spirit of another person, that is to say, the spirit of a wife, and subsequently the spirit of his children. The word groom can be defined as "one who is able to protect and make more attractive". In marriage, the husband is to cultivate, nourish, and protect the life of his wife like a garden. (Song of Solomon 4:12-16) He is to learn the art of cultivating land with the desire to make everything flourish, produce sweet fruit, and become a beautiful blossom. The calling of God for man is to be joined to his wife and become one spirit, a true reflection of Christ and the Church.

> **"Therefore a man shall leave his father and mother and be joined to his wife, and they shall become one flesh."**
>
> **Genesis 2:24**

The unity and success of a marriage requires a man with maturity, stability and strength of character. Many avoid marriage because this relationship demands the serious sacrifice of unwavering commitment and much responsibility. Many men would rather live the "playboy" fantasy lifestyle and constantly avoid the true commitment and responsibility, preferring to act like little boys. They meet, date, or loosely join in temporary relationships with multiple women but never have the capacity to be faithful to one. The ugly consequences of such selfish irresponsibility and childishness can cause devastating outcomes. Such a man will find himself in utter chaos: plundered, ruined, and stripped of all personal dignity and honor.

On the other hand, God calls every man to abandon his selfishness and deny himself from serving his own lust and personal cravings. God requires each man to defend, preserve, and guard the honor and dignity of a single marriage relationship. Man is to demonstrate that he is willing to lay down his life for the woman he loves and to protect her dignity by entering into the sacred covenant of marriage before the church altar. After a man has perfected his character as a husband by cultivating the spirit of his wife like a well-watered garden, he will see the flowers begin to blossom and bring forth precious fruit. Ultimately, he will reap a plentiful harvest of prosperity.

The following Biblical principles will help a man become a better husband: (<u>See.</u> 1 Peter 3:7)

⌘ Perfect the art of grooming or cultivating by guarding and nourishing his wife's body, soul, and spirit.

⌘ Take responsibility for himself and his wife. Rather than acting like her son, he is to lead her by following the example of Jesus Christ.

⌘ Avoid neglect, abuse, abandonment and all harshness or indifference.

⌘ Speak with gracious words learning to treat his wife with honor, understanding, and great discernment.

Fatherhood is the next step in man's progression toward maturity. To father children is a truly admirable and honorable phase in developing a man's character. To become a father is a challenge to further trust in God for provision, protection, and faithfulness, to serve the added offspring. Finding ways to honor God by raising children that love, serve and faithfully keep God's Word is a great challenge. Fatherhood becomes the gateway and rite of passage to the next generation who will inherit a legacy of God's blessing or the cursed consequences of an irresponsible male.

"...And the glory of children are their parents".
Proverbs 17:6

Children quickly realize whether their dad is a good husband or a negligent one, a dignified father or a shameful one. Their countenance loses brightness and many fall into depression when their fathers are unable to model manhood and preserve a healthy and cohesive family unit.

For this reason, it is essential that every man grow in his capacity to be a good husband and a father, worthy of being imitated by his children. He is to exemplify the character of Christ, nourish the triune nature of his children, and govern his household with the proper balance of love and discipline:

> *Deep inside each child's heart There is a longing to know and to say, "My dad loves my mom".*

"He who spares the rod hates his son, but he who loves him disciplines him promptly."
Proverbs 13:24

1. List three (3) ways a man must provide for his wife's physical, emotional, and spiritual needs?

   a._____

   b._____

   c._____

2. What can a man do in his marriage to cover his children with "glory" according to Proverbs 17:6?

SEGEMENT 3: PROVEN CHARACTER

Every man can grow by taking step after step toward manhood. Fisrt, a man is entrusted with the responsibility of his own spirit. Secondly he is responsible for his wife's spirit followed by his children's spirit, and finally a ministry to serve and care for the spirit of those outside of his own family namely: his local church. There are people who desire to become ministers of the gospel but do not understand that it requires great responsibility, maturity, faithfulness, stability, wisdom, and perseverance. A man must first prove that he can govern himself and his own household before he can be accountable for the work of God. As Paul instructs his young disciple Timothy in the following bible verse.

"For if a man does not know how to rule his own house, how will he take care of the church of God?"

I Timothy 3:5

Finally, God desires that every man manifest the likeness of Christ in true maturity. Jesus always led by example as he accepted the full responsibility of watching over His own spirit, then the spirit of his family and friends, and finally the Church. Through the Holy Spirit, Jesus offered himself up to provide salvation for the spirits of all men. Likewise, a faithful and mature man will show himself approved and demonstrate great leadership first in his own home. This commitment to properly lead his home will prepare a man to receive training to serve God in His church and the nations of the earth.

God reveals a principle in His word that a man who is faithful in the little things, can be entrusted over a greater measure and shoulder greater responsibilities. Since man was created in the likeness of God, he has been called to be like Jesus Christ and reach the stature, measure, and fullness of a perfect man.

The following points can be helpful reminders for a man who desires to present his character as perfect and improved before God.

1. Since man's personality is temporal and his character is eternal, it is worth while that man invest in developing his character instead of showcasing his personality.

2. In every situation a man must concern himself to take steps that are certain an upright, there is no room for hesitation, distraction, and instability.

3. Faithfulness and consistancy in responsibility are the hallmarks of a mature man.

4. A man is to love and lay down his life for his wife as Christ did for the Church.

5. A man who is to lead his family well will commit to cultivate, grow and govern himself, his wife, his children, and his ministry with the dignity of honor, integrity, and all wisdom.

> ***"His lord said to him, 'Well done, good and faithful servant; you have been faithful over a few things, I will make you ruler over many things. Enter into the joy of your lord."***
>
> ***Matthew. 25:23***

SELF-ASSESSMENT

1. Write down the secret rewards received by a each man as a result of their self-discipline in the following passages:

    a) 1 Samuel 3:13 _____

    b) 1 Kings 1:6 _____

    c) Proverbs 22:15 _____

    d) Proverbs 23:13-14 _____

    e) Proverbs 29:15 _____

    f) Hebrews 12:5-6 _____

2. Read: 1 Timothy 3:4-5 and 2 Timothy 2:2
In light of these two (2) verses, Write down the necessary and progressive steps a man must follow before he is able to lead a church ministry?

3. What seven (7) things can a man do to nourish and govern his own spirit?

   a. _____
   b. _____
   c. _____
   d. _____
   e. _____
   f. _____
   g. _____

4. What words described a man who governs his own spirit that suggest he has governed his spirit well?

5. Describe one (1) particular aspects of the weight of responsibility upon a man and how he needs to prepare to shoulder such weight.

6. True or False
As a man takes each step toward maturity, his level of responsibility as a (a) man, (b) husband, (c) father and (d) servant of God, grows in greater and greater weight and proportion.

True_____ False_____

Be prepared to share some of these answers in the next small group meeting.

GROUP MEETING (1 hour):

⌘ **WELCOME & PRAYER** (5 min): Begin by welcoming everyone and open in prayer asking God to reveal each man's responsibility to cultivate and govern his own spirit including that of his wife, children and church.

⌘ **LEADER'S NOTES** (15 min): Leader will share from his notes taken during the three (3) segments and re-read the related scripture verse(s) found in What is a Man? Chapter 7 (Prov. 3:35, 13:24, 17:6; 25:28; Psalms 8:3-6, 100:3, 101:6; Eph. 4:14, 1 Kings 1:5-6; 1 Cor. 13:11; Mt. 11:16, 25:23; Gen.2:24; 1 Pet. 3:7; 1 Tim. 3:5-6; 2 Tim. 2:2, Col. 1:15).

⌘ **DISCUSSION** (20 min): Each man will be invited to share their own notes and begin open dialogue with thoughts concerning the first 3 segments.

⌘ **ASSESSMENT** (15 min): Leader will read the questions from the "SELF-ASSESMENT" section and invite the men in the small group to share their answers with the rest of the group.

⌘ **PRAYER** (5 min): The meeting will conclude with a final prayer asking God for the courage and favor to grow in God's grace to take on the next level of responsibility as a man, husband, father, and servant of God.

SESSION VIII

FINALLY A MAN

In this session, the small group will focus upon the following aspects:

- Summarize the stages of a man's growth and development using Jesus Christ as the model and blueprint.

- Understand the importance and characteristics of a faithful son

- Consider the proper exercise of authority in a man's life

OVERVIEW

"Imitate me, just as I also imitate Christ."

1 Corinthians 11:1

Christ is the perfect and ultimate model of a true man who changed the world. Only Jesus example can lead a man to maturity and it is through the power of the Holy Spirit that every man is able to grow towards the full and perfect measure of Christ. Those who accept this challenge will refuse to quit until the character of Christ is entirely formed in them. Many times the apostle Paul admonished his followers regarding Christ being formed inside of them as God's ultimate plan.

"To them God willed to make known what are the riches of the glory of this mystery among the Gentiles: which is Christ in you, the hope of glory."

Colossians 1:27

"My little children, of whom I travail in birth again until Christ be formed in you."

Galatians 4:19

The secret pathway to becoming a man who can change the world is found in the Holy Bible as revealed in the life of Jesus Christ. The following Old Testament passage in Isaiah reveals a step-by-step progression for every man to reach true manhood in God's purpose.

"For unto us a Child is born, unto us a Son is given; and the government will be upon His shoulder. And His name will be called Wonderful, Counselor, Mighty God, Everlasting Father, and Prince of Peace. Of the increase of His government and peace there will be no end, upon the throne of David and over His kingdom, to order it and establish it with judgment and justice from that time forward, even forever. The zeal of the Lord of hosts will perform this."

Isaiah 9:6-7

Each step in this passage reveals the footsteps taken by Jesus Christ during his life to fulfill his charge as a man. Thus, in order to achieve true manhood, one can follow each step taken, and thus imitate Jesus' example. The prophet Isaiah foretold the coming of the greatest man to ever live upon the earth. The description of this true champion is announced as a forerunner for any man who desires to achieve perfect character. This passage so accurately summarizes the Biblical model of the journey to manhood that men are without excuse. This carefully written revelation opens a progressive rite of passage from one stage to the next to become a true champion:

1. "a Child is born"
2. "a Son is given"
3. "The government will be upon His shoulder"
4. "His name will be called Wonderful"
5. "Counselor, Mighty God, Everlasting Father, Prince of Peace"
6. "Prince of Peace"
7. "The increase of his government and peace there shall be no end."

PERSONAL QUEST

SEGMENT 1: FROM CHILDHOOD TO SONSHIP

The first stage toward the quest to manhood begins with childhood. Being a male is determined at birth, but manhood comes through the process of maturity. As studied before, a child has certain behaviors suitable for his age (1 Corinthians 13:11). However, as a child begins to grow, he must understand that the crowning achievement of manhood is accomplished through the suffering pathway of becoming a faithful son. A child must no longer seek the nurture of his mother alone, but should be trained under the tutelage of a father figure. Here a man learns to deny himself and walk in obedience, discipline, and correction within the framework of a father's love, trust, and protection. (See. Proverbs. 22:6 and Hebrews 12:7-8). As a man studies the life of Jesus Christ, he will notice how Jesus learned obedience by the things he suffered always trusting and pleasing His Heavenly Father. (John 8:29)

> A man's prosperity and future success depends on his development as a son; whether or not he was obedient and honoring and can therefore be trusted to carry the weight of greater responsibility.

Those who resist correction, resent a father's instruction, and continually try to side skirt discipline will ruin any possibility they might have of attaining the standard of sonship and therefore these men will impede and sabotage their own progress toward manhood.

"Though He was a Son, yet he learned obedience by the things which He suffered".
Hebrews 5:8

When a man becomes an obedient son, his father can trust him with the weight of greater responsibility. In today's culture, one frequently sees young men who refuse to partake in a relationship that honors their father. Many young men prefer to wander through life without a father's direction and choose to dodge accountability or instruction of any kind, forgoing obedience, and resenting commitment to personal responsibility. Those who desire to reach full maturity, blessing, and true prosperity are willing to bear the weight of responsibility and give account for his time, talents, and treasure with courage, submission and unwavering determination.

Subsequently, after a son allows himself to be instructed, corrected, and disciplined in a paternal relationship by accepting responsibility, he will receive a good name.

"A good name is to be chosen rather than great riches, loving favor rather than silver and gold."

Proverbs 22:1

Men who refuse the discipline of correction as sons and refuse to welcome the sufferings of a father's rebuke, admonition, and instruction become sons destined to shame and disgrace. These rebellious sons lack the necessary character to harness their emotional lust and for this reason they are unable to act responsibly, show honor, or restrain their disrespect. On the contrary, a faithful son is one who desires to imitate his father, accepting correction, and learns the pathway of obedience that leads to honor and success.

Through this process, a deligent son will develop and mature as a man to reach the maximum expression of his manhood and receive his God given reward.

"Children, obey your parents in the Lord, for this is right. "Honor your father and mother," which is the first commandment with promise: "that it may be well with you and you may live long on the earth."

Ephesians 6:1-3

1. Upon reading 1 Corinthians 13:11, the Bible reveals that at the center of a child's universe is himself as seen through three expressions. What are these three (3) visible expression of selfishness in a child?

   a. _____

   b. _____

   c. _____

2. Give three (3) examples of honor, suffering and obedience a son will face before he becomes a great man.

   a. _____

   b. _____

   c. _____

3. Name five (5) blessings or rewards that will come to an obedient son in this life?

   a. _____

   b. _____

   c. _____

   d. _____

   e. _____

4. Read: Proverbs 22:6, Ephesians 6:4
Name two (2) responsibilities of a father according to these Scriptures?

   a. _____

   b. _____

SEGMENT 2: A MATURE MAN

The next step in the process of becoming a man is the willingness to take a greater weight and yoke of responsibility. Many men are under the deception that life must be devoid of suffering and pleasure seeking becomes the ultimate goal. When a man decides to deny himself, he is now available to pursue the father's pleasure with various tasks to faithfully obey his father's instructions. In this process a man begins to properly invest his time by using his unique talents and abilities to reveal his leadership capacity. For the rest of his life, a man will be challenged daily to become a better husband to his wife, a champion father to his children, a blessing to his family, a faithful member of his church, and a patriarch to the nations. The Bible demonstrates this amazing journey in the life of Joseph who later became a man of great influence and a noble prince in Egypt. The early years of suffering and adverse hardship prepared him to be recognized in his latter years as a "father to Pharaoh."

"So now it was not you who sent me here, but God; and He has made me a father to Pharaoh, and lord of all his house, and a ruler throughout all the land of Egypt."

Genesis 45:8

In today's culture, it seems young men are more and more reluctant to accept commitment of any kind. They rather wander through life with peers that have no purpose or direction. However, only those courageous enough to welcome the challange of greater weight of responsibility will succeed toward a good future in a prominent name having honor.

Once a man is able to establish a faithful character he shall be given a name or reputation like Christ, such as "His name will be called Wonderful, Counselor, Mighty God, Everlasting Father, Prince of Peace." At this point a man is ready for marriage. The desire to establish his own home and family by entering into the covenant of marriage becomes the real evidence of his maturity. The ability to spread a respectful garment to cover a woman by giving and keeping his word in marriage before God to his bride begins a journey of greater weight of responsibility. In this stage, he will vow and be charged to love, protect, and provide for his wife within the holy state of marriage. By giving her his surname, he is committing to be her covering at all times in every area that he may present her before the Lord as a glorious bride: holy and without blemish.

> **When I passed by you again and saw you, behold, you were at the age for love, and I spread the corner of my garment over you and covered your nakedness; I made my vow to you and entered into a covenant with you, declares the Lord GOD, and you became mine."**
>
> **Ezekiel 16:8**

Then, as a man continues to be molded and perfected in his character, he will obtain greater knowledge, maturity, and wisdom to live as God has ordained. He will continue to grow and enjoy the manifold grace of God until he becomes a father. His ability to reproduce has the great purpose of raising, forming, and perfecting sons and daughters who in turn will also one day fulfill the purposes of God. God desires that a every man learn and become more fruitful and multiply and bring many sons to glory (Hebrews 2:10; Matthew 25:23).

1. List three (3) areas where a father can train his son by placing greater weight of responsibility to prepare him to be a great husband and father.

   a. _____
   b. _____
   c. _____

2. Read: Proverbs 22:1
Describe five (5) words associated with a man developing a "good name."

   a. _____
   b. _____
   c. _____
   d. _____
   e. _____

3. What **spiritual** and **physical** preparations should a man have in place as evidence of his mature character so when he finds a woman they could enter into the Holy Covenant of Marriage with a solid foundation?

Spiritual

a- _____
b- _____
c- _____
d- _____
e- _____

Physical

a- _____
b- _____
c- _____
d- _____
e- _____

SEGMENT 3: TO GOVERN WELL

"Of the increase of His government and peace there will be no end..."

Isaiah 9:6-7

This portion of Scripture reveals that maturity is an ongoing process. God continues to entrust a man with greater privilege of spiritual authority and anointing to lead the nations to the degree he is willing to grow in accepting more and more responsibility. God has called man to lead the nations that includes serving every people, tribe, and tongue. A real man will lead by example so that all peoples follow him as he renders true spiritual worship by honoring and praising God as the Supreme King of Glory. Since the beginning of time, God intended for man to walk before Him crowned with glory and honor:

"For You have made him a little lower than the angels, and You have crowned him with glory and honor."

Psalm 8:5

Sadly, very few men ever experience the reality of great splendor, glory, and honor of being crowned by God's favor in this life. However, those who do accept the challenge to answer this high call by accepting the responsibility to serve their generation and pursue the will of God with a vision to change the world will be greatly rewarded! This is the reason the apostle Paul made Christ his highest priority.

"Brethren, I do not count myself to have apprehended; but one thing I do, forgetting those things which are behind and reaching forward to those things which are ahead, I press toward the goal for the prize of the upward call of God in Christ Jesus."

Philippians 3:13-14

1. Name several character attributes that a man will need to lead his family, (wife and children) to a blessed, fruitful, and peaceful life.

2. Find four (4) Bible verses for each stage of a man's life? (i.e. a verse related to (1) son, (2) husband, (3) fathers, and lastly (4) patriarch.)

   a. _____

   b. _____

   c. _____

   d. _____

3. If glory and honor are God's plan to crown a faithful man than what are the opposite words that describe a man who loses his crown?

   a. _____

   b. _____

4. Read Philippians 3:13-14
Since perseverance is the foundation for every man to run and win in the race toward manhood, what advice would you give a man to encourage him to move forward and not give up?

Be prepared to share some of these answers in the next small group meeting.

SELF-ASSESSMENT

After completing the last three (3) segments, take some time to answer the following questions:

1. Read I Corinthians 13:4-8.

What words would describe the character of a man who reaches full maturity in manhood?

2. How does God show compassion for a man? (Romans 5:8)

3. How does a man demonstrate unconditional love and compassion to a friend, wife, or family member?

Be prepared to share some of these answers in the next small group meeting.

GROUP MEETING (1 hour):

⌘ **WELCOME & PRAYER** (5 min): Begin by welcoming each man and pray that God will open their eyes so they may see a clear progression toward maturity from childhood through son ship into a manhood that is able to grow and carry the weight of responsibility to be a blessing to his family by serving his wife and children.

⌘ **LEADER'S NOTES** (15 min): Leader will share from his notes taken during the three (3) segments and re-read the related scripture verse(s) found in What is a Man? Chapter 8 as time allows (Col. 1:27; Gal. 4:19; Is.9:6-7; Ezekiel 16:8, 1Cor.13:11; Ecc. 10:16; Prov. 18:22, 22:1,6; Heb. 5:8, 12:7-8; Eph. 6:1-3; Gen. 2:24, 45:8; James 3:2, 16; 1 Cor. 11:1, Phil. 3:13; Ps. 8:5).

⌘ **DISCUSSION** (20 min): Each man will be invited to share their own notes and begin open dialogue with thoughts concerning the first 3 segments.

⌘ **ASSESSMENT** (15 min): Leader will read the questions from the "SELF-ASSESMENT" section and invite the men in the small group to share their answers with the rest of the group.

⌘ **PRAYER** (5 min): The meeting will conclude with a final prayer asking God to lead each man in Christ's example as found in Isaiah 9:6 through each progressive rite of passage, from one stage to the next to become a true champion, with the help from the Holy Spirit as they press on toward the goal for the prize of the upward call of God in Christ Jesus as a faithful son, man, husband, father, and world changing man of God.

SESSION 9

LOVE VS. SELF

In this session, the small group will focus upon the following aspects:

- Learn the difference between the expression of love, empathy, and compassion.

- Identify the self-centered character and the expression of a selfish man.

- Respond to the final challenge of self-denial by walking in genuine love.

OVERVIEW

"Watch therefore, stand firm in the faith; be brave men, be strong; let all your things be done in love."

1 Corinthians 16:13-14

The courage, strength, and perseverance of a man are seldom thought as coming from the wellspring and essence of love. If the truth be known, the greatest of man's virtues find their origins in love. The presence of genuine love equips and prepares a man to confront any predicament or opposition that comes against him. Love serves as the greatest fuel for fulfilling the call to manhood. This love, however, can only be found and expressed through a personal and intimate relationship with the ultimate essence of love: Jesus Christ. Jesus came to earth with the exclusive purpose of manifesting the Father's love by laying his life down for others. He was moved by the Father's love to come seek and save lost man. His heartfelt-felt love for mankind was expressed through his continual compassion and selflessness towards others.

"Greater love has no one than this, than to lay down one's life for his friends."

John 15:13

When a man is willing to imitate and follow Christ's love, he will put an end to every immature and self-centered expression. His life will no longer produce selfish conduct that contradicts and hinders true manhood. The end result will be a habitual demonstration of genuine concern and compassion toward everyone around him. In fact, the value and significance of a man in the kingdom of God will depend on his capacity to love others with genuine love that can only be found in God.

"Though I speak with the tongues of men and of angels, but have not love, I have become sounding brass or a clanging cymbal. And though I have the gift of prophecy, and understand all mysteries and all knowledge, and though I have all faith, so that I could remove mountains, but have not love, I am nothing."

1 Corinthians 13:1-2

1. Reflect on today's cultural understanding of romantic love and how it distorts, confuses, and contradicts God's love and man's ability to express genuine love for others.

2. Describe the depth of a man's virtue when it is expressed through love.
   Begin with the following virtues: "strength, courage, perseverance, commitment, and loyalty."

3. How does perfecting a man's capacity to love help him become a better man, husband, and father.

4. What is the essence of love that men can imitate and follow as an example of perfect love.

5. What is the ultimate expression of darkness that diminishes a man's capacity to love others?

WHAT IS A MAN? Workbook

SEGMENT 1: AGAPE LOVE

"Love suffers long and is kind; love does not envy; love does not parade itself, is not puffed up; does not behave rudely, does not seek its own, is not provoked, thinks no evil; does not rejoice in iniquity, but rejoices in the truth; bears all things, believes all things, hopes all things, endures all things. Love never fails..."
1 Corinthians 13:4-8a

The essence of Christ is love. Therefore, man is to love others fully, absolutely, and selflessly through every situation and circumstance. God desires man to grow up with the capacity to respond in love towards others with true compassion. Sobriety, equilibrium, and honor become the hallmarks of a man who can interact and form healthy relationships with his family, community, church, city, and at every national level.

Love is the only hope for mankind. On occasion, God will allow men to have the opportunity to experience sacrificial love and thus experience true life. God's single most desire for man is that he grows in his capacity to express genuine love toward God and toward others. (Matthew 22:35-40). When love becomes the true motive for a man's every action it will lead his steps to continual victory. This love is perfected in each individual as they learn to deny themselves, show genuine concern for others, and express empathy and compassion that leads to Christ-likeness.

> A true man can be measured by his capacity to love and act without selfishness.

"That Christ may dwell in your hearts through faith; that you, being rooted and grounded in love, may be able to comprehend with all the saints what is the width and length and depth and height— to know the love of Christ which passes knowledge; that you may be filled with all the fullness of God."
Ephesians 3:17-19

1. Name Three (3) persons a man could purpose to demonstrate unselfish acts of love each day.

   a. _____

   b. _____

   c. _____

2. Read Matthew 22:35-40.
Explain why genuine love for God and for others should become a man's greatest pursuit.

3. List five (5) examples of how a man's love can be sharpened, perfected, and increased as his actions show less and less selfishness.

   a. _____

   b. _____

   c. _____

   d. _____

   e. _____

SEGMENT 2: LEAVING SELFISHNESS BEHIND

"For where envy and self-seeking exist, confusion and every evil thing are there."

James 3:16

When man decides to remove himself far from others, he becomes so isolated he can serve no one but himself. Selfish men are rotten to the core and carry the Devil's D.N.A. These men serve the satanic trilogy of, "Me. Myself and I.", becoming the most dangerous men upon the earth because they pursue their own desires, ambitions, and lusts at any cost and at the expense of others. Such men are incapable of demonstrating love, empathy, or compassion.

"A man who isolates himself seeks his own desire; he rages against all wise judgment."

Proverbs 18:1

Compassion is derived from the Latin word cumpassio, which literally means, "to share in the suffering or the pain of others." God is full of compassion for humanity. He manifests this through His intervention and participation in man's reality: He comes along side of man to meet his needs, comfort him, and helps carry his burdens.

> Compassion goes further than empathy because it is accompanied by the desire to alleviate or reduce the person's suffering

The difference between a mature man and an immature man is revealed at the moment that he is able to manifest a character that can show compassion and empathy. These are sentiments provoked by love that produces the healthy emotions and response that causes a man to act on behalf of those in need. However, when a man is unable to express compassion or empathy for others in their time of need or affliction it is because his heart has become callous and selfishness results in immaturity even if it is excused by indifference or oversight.

The Bible instructs each man to pursue a genuine relationship with God and with others through the bond of unity, namely God's love. He desires that man would live in unity with others by laying down his life of selfishness and exchange it for love and compassion. When a man is able to mature, he expresses an attitude of complete surrender before the needs of others. Genuine love eliminates a man's desire to act solely based on his own personal fears, feelings, or desires. As each man learns to deny himself and refuse to pursue his own personal ambition, he will become a great blessing to his friends, family, and the church. At this moment, the heavens are opened and God begins to pour out to this man the endless resources to meet all his needs by supplying according to His riches in glory and wealth in Christ Jesus. See. Philippians 4:19.

"That there should be no schism in the body, but that the members should have the same care for one another. And if one member suffers, all the members suffer with it; or if one member is honored, all the members rejoice with it."
1 Corinthians 12:25-26

1. What is God's antidote for man's selfishness?

2. List five (5) words that can describe a man who follows Christ's character when expressing God's love.

    a. _____

    b. _____

    c. _____

    d. _____

    e. _____

3. List five (5) words that can describe a man who follows Satan's character when expressing the Devil's selfishness.

   a. _____

   b. _____

   c. _____

   d. _____

   e. _____

4. Who are the first five (5) people who are directly impacted by a man who decides to pursue genuine love and compassion?

   a. _____

   b. _____

   c. _____

   d. _____

   e. _____

SEGMENT 3: LOVE NEVER FAILS

"LOVE NEVER FAILS..."
1 Corinthians 13:8a

For a man to follow in Christ's example, he must to accept an invitation to become a martyr. In other words, becoming a true man is to prepare to die for what you most love. The reason loves never fails is because it is unwilling to surrender and stands to endure any opposition. A true man is willing to follow Christ on the highest path of love. Following Christ means a man is willing to pursue heaven's most excellent virtue. The true test of manhood is taking the garments of Christ's love and accepting the battle armor of being clothed with humility to overcome life's greatest conflicts. Many men choose to surrender and run away not being able to suffer hardship, offense, and insult. Being able to utter the words, "Not my will but thy will be done" becomes man's challenge. Pride will always diminish a man's capacity to love. Genuine love has a high cost because a man will lose personal time, his schedule will be interrupted, life becomes messy and unpredictable, unmanageable, an expression of continual sacrifice to meet the needs and priorities of others. Walking in God's love will require a man to pay this high price. The following passage is an example of God paying a high price for the object of His love.

"God so loved the world, that he gave his only Son, that whoever believes in him should not perish but have eternal life."
John 3:16

A love like God's love is not easily overcome but sufficient enough to arm any man with the serious power and tenacity to overcome any adversity. This love is not superficial and whimsical but deep, committed and long-suffering. God's love is willing to pay the highest price, sail the widest ocean and climb the highest mountain. When the love of God has been perfected in a man he is able to pursue his highest call to serve and surrender to those he most dearly loves.

Eternity will be a dwelling place where the endless expression of God's love is experienced and shared. God's plan from the very beginning for man was for him to abide in the full expression of God's love. When genuine love is no longer man's reality every foundation for his existence is broken and he is rendered unable to build any lasting or meaningful relationship. Only God's love in man's heart is able to direct his steps to lasting significant and purpose. God's love in the schoolhouse of life will educate and train a man to become a blessing and not a menace or curse to society.

> ***"But whosoever keeps his word, in him verily is the love of God perfected: hereby know we that we are in him."***
>
> ***1 John 2:5***

While a man may pursue after many other priorities during his journey upon the earth, only the love of God will sustain and allow him to succeed in lasting genuine prosperity. To be able to exercise genuine love and not fall victim to the counterfeit expressions become a man's real challenge. If falling prey to the selfishness of others is able to wreak havoc in people's lives imagine finding a man at the whim and discretion of his own personal selfishness. The prodigal son becomes a good example for those men who choose to fall away and into the tragedy of "selfishness" as a way of life. Choosing to live outside the perfected love of God in obedience to His Word will subject a man to a nightmare of continual destruction and loss. Without God's love man finds himself falling into the quagmire of becoming a self-centered pig. The only remedy to this awful plight is to return and seeks to imitate the father's love in a genuine relationship of obedience that is willing to cares for others.

> ***"I will arise and go to my father, and will say to him, "Father, I have sinned against heaven and before you, and I am no longer worthy to be called your son. Make me like one of your hired servants."***
>
> ***Luke 15:18-19***

Many men complain that in "theory" the concept of God's love to overcome controversy is fantastic, however the theory runs in to problems in the midst of battle when the love fest is over and insults begin to fly. The real question men have is "where can I get a refill?" to refuel for the next round of life's difficult challenges. The following Scripture verse is able to assist a man in getting another dose of God's love from the Holy Ghost.

"Now hope does not disappoint, because <u>the love of God has been poured out in our hearts</u> by the Holy Spirit who was given to us."

Romans 5:5

1. Both a strong faith and an unwavering hope are necessary to keep a man from falling into the pit of immaturity, but what is the single most powerful character attribute a man must display to show forth strength, depth and long-term maturity as a man?

2. Read Proverbs 16:6-7 and explain the following phrase.
"When a man decides to live as a true expression of love he will outlast any problem and outlive all his enemies."

3. Read 1 John 2:5
When a man obeys God's Word his love is perfected in what ways?

4. Read Hebrews 13:5
Explain, "love never fails" in the context of marriage and family.

5. In your own words write down the meaning of Romans 5:5, that points a man to the Holy Spirit as the source & fountain of God's love so that he can continue overcoming the hardships and tribulations of loving difficult people in difficult times.

6. Read Galatians 5:22
Explain how a man can benefit from the fruit of the Spirit so he can love and serve his family and others.

SELF-ASSESSMENT

After completing the last three (3) segments, take some time answer the following questions:

1. Describe genuine love with as many words as you can recall from 1 Corinthians 13:1-8

   a. _____   e. _____
   b. _____   f. _____
   c. _____   g. _____
   d. _____   h. _____

2. In what ways has God shown compassion in your life?

3. Describe an opportunity that you currently have to demonstrate unconditional love and compassion to a friend or family member?

Be prepared to share some of your answers in the next small group meeting.

GROUP MEETING (1 hour):

⌘ **WELCOME & PRAYER** (5 min): Begin by welcoming every man and open in prayer asking God to reveal and empower men to demonstrate compassion and be motivated by genuine love to serve others.

⌘ **LEADER'S NOTES** (15 min): Leader will share from his notes taken during the three (3) segments and re-read the related scripture verse(s) found in What is a Man? Chapter 9 as time allows (Eph. 3:17-19; Mt. 22:35-40; James 3:16; Prov. 18:1; 1 Cor. 12:25-26; 13:1-14; John 15:13, 1 Corinthians 13:8a, John 3:16, 1 John 2:5, Luke 15:18-19, Romans 5:5, Galatians 5:22).

⌘ **DISCUSSION** (20 min): Each man will be invited to share their own notes and begin open dialogue with thoughts concerning the first 3 segments.

⌘ **ASSESSMENT** (15 min): Leader will read the questions from the "SELF-ASSESMENT" section and invite the men in the small group to share their answers with the rest of the group.

⌘ **PRAYER** (5 min): The meeting will conclude with prayer asking God to fill each man with His Holy Spirit and love as they accept the charge to grow, show and demonstrate compassion by walking in genuine love.

CONCLUSION

How exciting to know that every man can achieve God's calling to become like Christ! This is not a purely intellectual, philosophical, or religious calling, but rather an invitation to walk in that reality each day imitating Jesus. The transformation into Christ's image is both a glorious opportunity and a serious challenge that can be attained through God's amazing grace. (Titus 2:11-14) Small steps of obedience, honor, and courage mark the journey from childhood to patriarch.

Every man ought to know that the opposite of destruction is instruction. A wise man that is careful to heed God's counsel will avoid the irreparable ruins of a lifetime and cling to God's promises for prosperity enjoying great success. Such a man will choose his companions wisely and allow the Holy Spirit to carefully guide him to a healthy spiritual fellowship. Finally, a mature man will have the confidence of knowing that every warrior can prepare for war, but it is God who delivers him to obtain lasting victory. In this journey toward manhood, a man's confidence to overcome every obstacle, fear, and uncertainty, shall be the promise of God's Word that declares, "He who began a good work in you shall be faithful" to complete it!

"Being confident of this very thing, that He who has begun a good work in you will complete it until the day of Jesus Christ..."
Philippians 1:6

Some key points to remember are as follows:

1. A true man demonstrates his love toward others by constantly serving and pouring out his life to embrace the needs, hurts, and pains of those around him.

2. A man's code for conduct and life is to walk in honor, obedience, and selflessness.

3. A man is to exhibit solidarity of purpose, a positive attitude, generosity, and self-denial at all times.

4. A man must abhor the expression of inconsiderate, greedy, selfish ambition, and lack of integrity.
See. Hebrews 1:9

5. A man is able to stands firm and conduct himself valiantly, by fully surrendering to God, and always live motivated by God's love

There is one last piece of advice for those desiring to make a difference and change the world: seek the companionship of like-minded men. God instructs true man to walk in the company of wise men and avoid the company of fools (Prov. 13:20; Ps. 1:1; 1 Cor. 15:33).

The Apostle Paul warned the Corinthians people that a man's character can be altered and would be corrupted to the point of undergoing serious adverse change solely from the company he and draws near to and keeps.

"Do not be so deceived and misled, wrong companionship, communion, and associations corrupt and deprave good manners, morals, and character."

1 Corinthians 15:33

The quest to manhood is both a challenging and exciting journey. This pursuit is designed by God to carry all men to the full, stature, and measure of His Son, Jesus Christ. From childhood to patriarch, a man must allow God to mold him, guide him, guard him and fulfill His purpose in life. A man must know with full confidence that God is able to sustain every man through each stage of life's journey. God the Father, the Son, and the Holy Spirit can fill a man with amazing wisdom, grace, mercy, and power to follows in the example of Christ. This transformation will continue until the image of Christ is formed in man for the glory and honor of God.

"For whom He foreknew, He also predestined to be conformed to the image of His Son, that He might be the firstborn among many brethren."

Romans 8:29

FINAL CONCLUSION

1. Read Proverbs 13:20.
How can selecting the fellowship and company of wise men help a man's quest for maturity and true manhood?

2. Read Proverbs 21:31.
Write down the advice for a man to trust God for the final outcome.

3. Read Job 42:10.
Pray to God that your small group companions will continue to grow into true men by learning and living the principles found in the "What is a man?" book.

4. Write a small note to a friend and a one-sentence e-mail with a thought that summarizes what God has done through the "What is a man?" series and workbook quest.

5. Visit the "What is a Man?" website (www.whatisaman.com) and share your heart on how this workbook series, touched and transformed your life including any significant testimony on the tools God has given to accomplish this challenge as an encouragement to other men.

6. DECLARATION OF MANHOOD

I,_____, declare today that:
(Insert your name here)

I accept full responsibility for my life and I will make decisions based on sound judgment in according to God's word. I acknowledge that God has given me His Word, His Spirit, and His grace, and these are sufficient to guide me in taking my next steps.

I am an integral part of His church, and His authority keeps my back at all times. I renounce excuses and refuse to blame others for my mistakes; forgetting those things, which are behind, and reaching forward to those things, which are ahead.

I will respond to the high calling of God to be a true man in all fullness of maturity, in the name of Jesus Christ, and for His glory.

LEADER NOTES

"And the things that you have heard from me among many witnesses, commit these to faithful men who will be able to teach others also."

2 Timothy 2:2

As a group leader, you will help facilitate a discussion about the topic of the week, review and explain relevant scriptures, and challenge small group members to respond to the week's challenge.

Some helpful tips are as follows:
- Make every effort to be respectful of people's time by starting and ending each meeting on a timely basis.
- Each week begin by introducing each man in your small group to one another to break the ice and create an atmosphere where men are comfortable to open up with each other.
- Study the overview for each topic and take time to complete the three (3) segments for each week.
- Use the notes you took throughout the week as a guide for the discussion. The notes should not be read out loud during the class. Rather, the leader should be prepared to share these principles and help each group member understand how to apply them.
- Read all the verses included in each lesson and look up the references for additional verses found in the corresponding chapters in the "What is a man?" book.
- Emphasize the importance of studying the Bible and the fruit it produces in the life of a man.
- Avoid saying, "Okay?" or "Amen?" after every sentence. Instead use the questions from the "self-assessment" sections to make sure small group members understand the material.
- Avoid belittling or embarrassing someone who does not answer correctly. Do, however, re-state the truth and remind them of the scriptures where it is found. Provide additional examples or verses to make sure everyone understands.
- Address any misconceptions as they arise during the meeting with a firm but merciful attitude.
- Remember to begin and end each session in prayer and spend time praying for each man of your small group during the week.
- Expect God to do big things and move in amazing ways!

SMALL GROUP DIRECTORY

Write your name on this page. Pass your books around and ask the Small Group members to fill in their names and contact information in each other's books.

YOUR NAME: _____

Name: _____ Name: _____
Home Phone: _____ Home Phone: _____
Mobile Phone: _____ Mobile Phone: _____
E-Mail: _____ E-Mail: _____
Social Network(s): _____ Social Network(s): _____

Name: _____ Name: _____
Home Phone: _____ Home Phone: _____
Mobile Phone: _____ Mobile Phone: _____
E-Mail: _____ E-Mail: _____
Social Network(s): _____ Social Network(s): _____

Name: _____ Name: _____
Home Phone: _____ Home Phone: _____
Mobile Phone: _____ Mobile Phone: _____
E-Mail: _____ E-Mail: _____
Social Network(s): _____ Social Network(s): _____

Name: _____ Name: _____
Home Phone: _____ Home Phone: _____
Mobile Phone: _____ Mobile Phone: _____
E-Mail: _____ E-Mail: _____
Social Network(s): _____ Social Network(s): _____

NOTES

NOTES

NOTES

NOTES

NOTES

NOTES